SELECTED POEMS

OF

THOMAS MERTON

SELECTED POEMS

OF

THOMAS MERTON

WITH AN INTRODUCTION BY

MARK VAN DOREN

A NEW DIRECTIONS PAPERBOOK

Library of Congress Catalog Card No. 59-15019

First Published as a New Directions
Paperbook Original (No. 85), 1959

Nihil Obstat

      EDWARD J. MONTANO, S.T.D.
      CENSOR LIBRORUM
Imprimatur

      ✠ FRANCIS CARDINAL SPELLMAN
      ARCHBISHOP OF NEW YORK

PS
3525
E7174
A17
1959

The nihil obstat and imprimatur are official declarations
that a book or pamphlet is free of doctrinal or moral error.
No implication is contained therein that those who have
granted the nihil obstat and imprimatur agree with the
contents, opinions or statements expressed.

Manufactured in the United States of America

New Directions Books are published by James Laughlin
New York Office—333 Sixth Avenue, New York 14

CONTENTS

INTRODUCTION
by
Mark Van Doren

INTRODUCTION

In the summer of 1953 Thomas Merton wrote to me from Gethsemani: "Our cow barn burned down in little over twenty minutes or half an hour—like a pile of brush. We could do nothing to put it out. Everybody thought it was a really beautiful fire, and it was. I am sending you a poem about it." The poem was "Elegy for the Monastery Barn," and I liked it so much that six years later, when I knew I was going to write this preface, I wrote Merton saying I hoped it would be among the poems he had selected. He replied: "I forget whether or not I included the Barn on the original list, perhaps I was shy about it. As a matter of fact it is for me subjectively an important poem, because when I was a kid on a farm in Maryland (yes, even that, for a while) a barn burned down in the middle of the night and it is one of the earliest things I can remember. So burning barns are for me great mysteries that are important. They turn out to be the whole world, and it is the Last Judgement."

Well, the poem is here, and it is as good a place as any to start looking at and listening to the poet in Thomas Merton. But one further document has a bearing on the subject. The preface to *The Strange Islands*, 1957, ends with these sentences: " 'Elegy for the Monastery Barn' was written after the cowbarn at Gethsemani burned down, one August evening in 1953, during the evening meditation. The monks left the meditation to fight a very hot fire and the poem arrived about the same time as the fire truck from the nearest town." The bearing is in the humor, which Merton never is without, and in the knowledge he keeps of the way things go in this world. The slowness of the truck, the swiftness of the poem, the childhood memory: all of these are somehow there, illuminating if not explaining the happy power awakened in Merton's mind as it races through the realities of his theme. For the burning barn is really an old lady dressed for her last hour in unaccountable finery, nor is any distinction to be made between her proud cries and the crackling of the flames. And she leaves us when she is gone with delicate memories of what she had been during the years when we ignored her: of her solitude, her peace, her patience as she waited for this end. The fifty invisible cattle, the fifty past years, are just as real; and so at the close is Merton's flight into another dimension where the Holy One sits in the presence of disaster. All is real; nothing is made up; this, we instantly believe, is the true content of the subject, which like any other subject starts on earth and gets in its own natural way to heaven.

Such, I take it, is what Merton means in the note on "Poetry and Contemplation" which he appends to the present volume. He says there, better he thinks than he did ten years ago, and in this I believe him to be right, that poetry at its best *is* contemplation—of things, and of what they signify. Not what they can be made to signify, but what they actually do signify, even when nobody knows it. The better the poet, the more we are convinced that he has knowledge of this kind, and has it humbly. "The earliest fathers," Merton wrote me in 1954, "knew that all things, as such, are symbolic by their very being and nature, and all talk of something beyond themselves. Their meaning is not something we impose upon them, but a mystery which we can discover in them, if we have the eyes to look with." The right eyes for the purpose are keen and honest, and there had better be some humor in them too. At least that is where poetry begins, whether its aim is religious or not. And certainly, if its aim is religious, it must begin there if it is ever to move us deeply. Religious poetry is rooted in things as much as any other kind of poetry is. Without that root it is merely pious, as its secular counterpart is merely poetical.

The sight and sound and feel of things is everywhere in Merton's poetry. Consider the first line of "Trappists, Working":

> Now all our saws sing holy sonnets in this
> world of timber.

The sound, so sudden and robust, brings with it a sense of the joy with which it is made, and the context of that joy. Perhaps there is no sound at all in the beginning lines of "The Trappist Cemetery—Gethsemani":

> Brothers, the curving grasses and their daughters
> Will never print your praises.

But no sound was intended; the prim alliteration in the second line is like a finger laid upon the lips, forbidding speech where no speech would be proper. The silence asked for here is nothing like the heavier sort that states itself in the first of "Three Postcards from the Monastery":

> The pilgrim passes swiftly.
> All the strange towns,
> Wrapped in their double cloaks
> (Of rain and of non-entity)
> Veil their elusive faces.

The wit of the parenthesis is no less deadly for being all but voiceless, as befits the faceless towns behind their veils of rain. What a plenitude of sound, however, comes to us out of eleven words in "The Trappist Abbey: Matins,"

> where some train runs, lost,
> Baying in eastward mysteries of distance.

And again it is true that the thing we hear speaks of more than itself; its skilful music is in the service of a thought so wide that all the world at dawn, near by and far away, is sleepily included. Elsewhere we read:

> But sound is never half so fair
> As when that music turns to air
> And the universe dies of excellence.

Those lines from "A Psalm" bring sound to a dead stop, drowned as it were in itself, and signifying by its very extinction the universe beyond sense.

Sight and sound and feeling. I have spoken so far only of sound, and indeed that may be enough, for in

the poetry of Thomas Merton all the senses work together to one end, the letting of things declare themselves. Which of the senses is dominant, for instance,
in this passage from "The Sowing of Meanings"?

> For, like a grain of fire
> Smouldering in the heart of every living essence
> God plants His undivided power—
> Buries His thought too vast for worlds
> In seed and root and blade and flower,
> Until, in the amazing light of April,
> Surcharging the religious silence of the spring,
> Creation finds the pressure of his everlasting
>   secret
> Too terrible to bear.
> Then everywhere we look, lo! rocks and trees
> Pastures and hills and streams and birds and
>   firmament
> And our own souls within us flash.

It is something to be seen and heard and felt in one
miraculous moment; also, to be wondered at and
contemplated, thought about and blissfully forgotten. Yet sound is somehow for Merton the carrying
sense, the medium through which experience of any
magnitude makes itself seen and felt. Of any magnitude—a reminder that Merton is a noticer of little
things as well as huge ones. Of children, for instance,
and their

> little voices, light as stems of lilies.

Are these voices heard or seen? Or felt? It does not matter, in view of the unearthly sweetness they signify, any more than it matters how we decide to explain the magic by which St. Agnes, with no thought of us in her small head, steals all our love as we behold her.

> Hear with what joy this child of God
> Plays in the perfect garden of her
>   martyrdom, . . .
> Spending the silver of her little life
> To bring her Bridegroom these bright flowers
> Of which her arms are full. . . .
> Her virtues, with their simple strings,
> Play to the Lover hidden in the universe.

The foregoing would suggest that the special reputation of Merton's poem "For My Brother: Reported Missing in Action, 1943" is not an accident. No poem in the book is better known, and the reason may lie in the music it makes. It is the kind of music that only poetry can make: not pure sound, of course, but something buried in the words and (in this case) mourning there. *The Seven-Storey Mountain* tells the story of the brother's death in prose that moves the reader too; without, however, assembling the sounds that are climaxed here in two paradoxical verses:

> The silence of Whose tears shall fall
> Like bells upon your alien tomb.

The poem, having created its own silence in preparation for these lines, drops them into our imagination where it is possible for tears that make no noise to sound nevertheless like delicate, distinct bronze, hopelessly far away. The figures of the poem are justly celebrated: the sleepless eyes as flowers, the fasts as willows, the thirst as springs, and the money of breath and death and weeping. Yet figures alone do not make a great poem. There must be a music that absorbs them and relates them, and gives them in the end a power for which we cannot assign the cause. We can say that the very intensity of the poet's fear that he will fail is somehow the reason for his success; we can guess that inarticulate grief manages here, simply because it must, to become articulate after all; but it is truer to say that in such a poem sadness sings—a low note, in perfect pitch, that carries around the world.

For Merton there is another world beyond this one where his brother died, and where he himself writes poetry. But the poetry is a way to that world. Indeed, given his endowment, is may well be *the* way, so that mystic and poet, seer and singer, in his case are one.

MARK VAN DOREN

SELECTED POEMS

OF

THOMAS MERTON

The windy

LENT IN A YEAR OF WAR

One of you is a major, made of cord and catskin,

But never dreams his eyes may come to life and thread
The needle-light of famine in a waterglass.

One of you is the paper Jack of Sprites
And will not cast his sentinel voice
Spiraling up the dark ears of the wind
Where the prisoner's yell is lost.

> "What if it was our thumbs put out the sun
> When the Lance and Cross made their mistake?
> You'll never rob us our Eden of drumskin shel-
> ters,
> You, with the bite of John the Baptist's halter,
> Getting away in the basket of Paul,
> Loving the answer of death, the mother of Lent!"

Thus, in the evening of their sinless murders,
Jack and the Major, sifting the stars for a sign
See the north-south horizon parting like a string!

3

THE FLIGHT INTO EGYPT

Through every precinct of the wintry city
Squadroned iron resounds upon the streets;
Herod's police
Make shudder the dark steps of the tenements
At the business about to be done.

Neither look back upon Thy starry country,
Nor hear what rumors crowd across the dark
Where blood runs down those holy walls,
Nor frame a childish blessing with Thy hand
Towards that fiery spiral of exulting souls!

Go, Child of God, upon the singing desert,
Where, with eyes of flame,
The roaming lion keeps thy road from harm.

SONG FOR OUR LADY OF COBRE

The white girls lift their heads like trees,
The black girls go
Reflected like flamingoes in the street.

The white girls sing as shrill as water,
The black girls talk as quiet as clay.

4

The white girls open their arms like clouds,
The black girls close their eyes like wings:
Angels bow down like bells,
Angels look up like toys,

Because the heavenly stars
Stand in a ring:
And all the pieces of the mosaic, earth,
Get up and fly away like birds.

THE NIGHT TRAIN

In the unreason of a rainy midnight
France blooms along the windows
Of my sleepy bathysphere,
And runs to seed in a luxuriance of curious lights.

Escape is drawn straight through my dream
And shines to Paris, clean as a violin string,
While spring tides of commotion,
(The third-class pianos of the Orient Express)
Fill the hollow barrels of my ears.

Cities that stood, by day, as gay as lancers
Are lost, in the night, like old men dying.
At a point where polished rails branch off forever
The steels lament, like crazy ladies.

5

We wake, and weep the deaths of the cathedrals
That we have never seen,
Because we hear the jugulars of the country
Fly in the wind, and vanish with a cry.

At once the diplomats start up, as white as bread,
Buckle the careless cases of their minds
That just fell open in the sleeper:

For, by the rockets of imaginary sieges
They see to read big, terrible print,
Each in the other's face,

That spells the undecoded names
Of the assassins they will recognise too late:
The ones that seem to be secret police,
Now all in place, all armed, in the obvious ambush.

SAINT JASON

This is the night the false Saint Jason
Wakes in fear from his cannibal sleep,
And drenches the edges of his eyes
With his tears' iron overflow;

For the flying scream of his dead woman
Opened the stitches of his skin,
And Jason bounced in the burly wind
Like a man of sack and string.

6

"What do you want, in the windows of your wound
Where Judas' money shines
By daggers' waterlight?"

"—I want the martyrs' eyes, as tight as shells,
In death's pretended sleep."

"What does it mean sunlight weeps in your door
Like an abandoned child?"

"—It means the heavyhanded storm,
Whirling and ploughing the wet woods,
Has filled with terrible speech
The stone doors of my feast:

The feast of the false Saint Jason's first communion."

THE MESSENGER

There is some sentry at the rim of winter
Fed with the speech the wind makes
In the grand belfries of the sleepless timber.

He understands the lasting strife of tears,
And the way the world is strung;
He waits to warn all life with the tongue of March's
    bugle,
Of the coming of the warrior sun.

When spring has garrisonned up her army of water,
A million grasses leave their tents, and stand in rows
To see their invincible brother.
Mending the winter's ruins with their laughter,
The flowers go out to their undestructive wars.

Walk in the woods and be witnesses,
You, the best of these poor children.

When Gabriel hit the bright shore of the world,
Yours were the eyes saw some
Star-sandalled stranger walk like lightning down the
        air,
The morning the Mother of God
Loved and dreaded the message of an angel.

THE REGRET

When cold November sits among the reeds like an un-
        lucky fisher

And ducks drum up as sudden as the wind
Out of the rushy river,
We slowly come, robbed of our rod and gun,
Walking amid the stricken cages of the trees.

The stormy weeks have all gone home like drunken
        hunters,
Leaving the gates of the grey world wide open to De-
        cember.

But now there is no speech of branches in these broken
    jails.
Acorns lie over the earth, no less neglected
Than our unrecognizable regret:
And here we stand as senseless as the oaks,
As dumb as elms.

And though we seem as grave as jailers, yet we did
    not come to wonder
Who picked the locks of the past days, and stole our
    summer.
(We are no longer listeners for curious saws, and
    secret keys!)

We are indifferent to seasons,
And stand like hills, deaf.
And never hear the last of the escaping year
Go ducking through the bended branches like a leaf.

AUBADE: LAKE ERIE

When sun, light handed, sows this Indian water
With a crop of cockles,
The vines arrange their tender shadows
In the sweet leafage of an artificial France.

Awake, in the frames of windows, innocent children,
Loving the blue, sprayed leaves of childish life,
Applaud the bearded corn, the bleeding grape,
And cry:

"Here is the hay-colored sun, our marvelous cousin,
Walking in the barley,
Turning the harrowed earth to growing bread,
And splicing the sweet, wounded vine.

Lift up your hitch-hiking heads
And no more fear the fever,
You fugitives, and sleepers in the fields,
Here is the hay-colored sun!"

And when their shining voices, clean as summer,
Play, like churchbells over the field,
A hundred dusty Luthers rise from the dead, un-
heeding,
Search the horizon for the gap-toothed grin of fac-
tories,
And grope, in the green wheat,
Toward the wood winds of the western freight.

POEM

Watching, among the rifled branches, for the sun, our
hero,
(Sing, wind, too tuneless in the slender trees)

We think about a whiter day, the marble temples
And the hills, our girls,

The even lovelier skies,
The horses of Poseidon, the lifting seas,
All grave, and clean, and wiser than the glassy morn-
           ings.

Watching, among the colored rocks, the sea, our happy
           swimmer,
(Sing, winds, more clearly on the Greek acropoli)

We think about the cries of drowners and the shine of
           armor,
While the hills, our citadels,
The strict, immovable trees,
   (More marble than the marching winner
   Who winters in our corridors of discontent)
Grow cloudy, in the teeth of the command.

Waiting, among the rifled temples for the light, our
           savior,
(Play, winds, in this too voiceless choir of columns)

We think about the whiter colonnades, the wiser city,
While the green hills, our shambles,
The burning olive gardens,
Have made the country blinder than the smoky tem-
           ples,
Louder and harsher than the foamy sea.

Waiting among the rifled branches for the sun, our
           hero,
Sing, wind, too tuneless in the slender trees!

FOR MY BROTHER:
REPORTED MISSING IN ACTION, 1943

Sweet brother, if I do not sleep
My eyes are flowers for your tomb;
And if I cannot eat my bread,
My fasts shall live like willows where you died.
If in the heat I find no water for my thirst,
My thirst shall turn to springs for you, poor traveller.

Where, in what desolate and smokey country,
Lies your poor body, lost and dead?
And in what landscape of disaster
Has your unhappy spirit lost its road?

Come, in my labor find a resting place
And in my sorrows lay your head,
Or rather take my life and blood
And buy yourself a better bed—
Or take my breath and take my death
And buy yourself a better rest.

When all the men of war are shot
And flags have fallen into dust,
Your cross and mine shall tell men still
Christ died on each, for both of us.

For in the wreckage of your April Christ lies slain,
And Christ weeps in the ruins of my spring:
The money of Whose tears shall fall
Into your weak and friendless hand,
And buy you back to your own land:

The silence of Whose tears shall fall
Like bells upon your alien tomb.
Hear them and come: they call you home.

THE WINTER'S NIGHT

When, in the dark, the frost cracks on the window
The children awaken, and whisper.
One says the moonlight grated like a skate
Across the freezing river.
Another hears the starlight breaking like a knifeblade
Upon the silent, steelbright pond.
They say the trees are stiller than the frozen water
From waiting for a shouting light, a heavenly mes-
    sage.

Yet it is far from Christmas, when a star
Sang in the pane, as brittle as their innocence!
For now the light of early Lent
Glitters upon the icy step—
"We have wept letters to our patron saints,
(The children say) yet slept before they ended."

Oh, is there in this night no sound of strings, of
    singers?
None coming from the wedding, no, nor Bride-
    groom's messenger?
(The sleepy virgins stir, and trim their lamps.)

The moonlight rings upon the ice as sudden as a
    footstep;
Starlight clinks upon the dooryard stone, too like a
    latch,
And the children are, again, awake,
And all call out in whispers to their guardian angels.

IN MEMORY OF THE SPANISH POET
FEDERICO GARCIA LORCA

Where the white bridge rears up its stamping arches
Proud as a colt across the clatter of the shallow river,
The sharp guitars
Have never forgotten your name.

Only the swordspeech of the cruel strings
Can pierce the minds of those who remain,
Sitting in the eyeless ruins of the houses,
The shelter of the broken wall.

A woman has begun to sing:
O music the color of olives!

14

Her eyes are darker than the deep cathedrals;
Her words come dressed as mourners,
In the gate of her shadowy voice,
Each with a meaning like a sheaf of seven blades!

The spires and high Giraldas, still as nails
Nailed in the four cross roads,
Watch where the song becomes the color of carna-
    tions,
And flowers like wounds in the white dust of Spain.

(Under what crossless Calvary lie your lost bones,
    Garcia Lorca?
What white Sierra hid your murder in a rocky val-
    ley?)

In the four quarters of the world, the wind is still,
And wonders at the swordplay of the fierce guitar;
The voice has turned to iron in the naked air,
More loud and more despairing than a ruined tower.

(Under what crossless Calvary lie your lost bones,
    Garcia Lorca?
What white Sierra hid your murder in a rocky val-
    ley?)

15

THE TRAPPIST ABBEY: MATINS

(Our Lady of Gethsemani, Kentucky)

When the full fields begin to smell of sunrise
And the valleys sing in their sleep,
The pilgrim moon pours over the solemn darkness
Her waterfalls of silence,
And then departs, up the long avenue of trees.

The stars hide, in the glade, their light, like tears,
And tremble where some train runs, lost,
Baying in eastward mysteries of distance,
Where fire flares, somewhere, over a sink of cities.

Now kindle in the windows of this ladyhouse, my
    soul,
Your childish, clear awakeness:
Burn in the country night
Your wise and sleepless lamp.
For, from the frowning tower, the windy belfry,
Sudden the bells come, bridegrooms,
And fill the echoing dark with love and fear.

Wake in the windows of Gethsemani, my soul, my
    sister,
For the past years, with smokey torches, come,
Bringing betrayal from the burning world
And bloodying the glade with pitch flame.

Wake in the cloisters of the lonely night, my soul, my
    sister,
Where the apostles gather, who were, one time, scat-
    tered,
And mourn God's blood in the place of His betrayal,
And weep with Peter at the triple cock-crow.

EVENING

Now, in the middle of the limpid evening,
The moon speaks clearly to the hill.
The wheatfields make their simple music,
Praise the quiet sky.

And down the road, the way the stars come home,
The cries of children
Play on the empty air, a mile or more,
And fall on our deserted hearing,
Clear as water.

They say the sky is made of glass,
They say the smiling moon's a bride.
They say they love the orchards and apple trees,
The trees, their innocent sisters, dressed in blossoms,
Still wearing, in the blurring dusk,
White dresses from that morning's first communion.

And, where blue heaven's fading fire last shines
They name the new come planets
With words that flower
On little voices, light as stems of lilies.

And where blue heaven's fading fire last shines,
Reflected in the poplar's ripple,
One little, wakeful bird
Sings like a shower.

ARIADNE AT THE LABYRINTH

Patient, in the fire of noon,
Hands, that hold the thread, crossed,
Ariadne's a Barbadian flower,
And grows by the Labyrinth door.

Under the blue, airy-waters of evening,
Hands folded like white petals,
Watching for the bold adventurer,
Ariadne waits as calm as coral,
Silent as some plant of undersea.

Drums ring at the city's edge:
The speechless hills put on crowns of dark flame;
Dancing citizens fly like little flags
Amid the glad volcano of their congas.
But Ariadne's eyes are lakes
Beside the maze's starwhite wall:

For in the Carribbean midnight
Of her wild and gentle wisdom, she foreknows
And solves the maze's cruel algebra.

But when white morning
Runs with a shout along the jagged mountains
Strength of a cotton thread draws out to Ariadne
The Bravest Soldier, the Wisest Judge,
The Mightiest King!

ST. AGNES: A RESPONSORY

Cujus pulchritudinem
Sol et luna mirantur . . .
    Hear with what joy this child of God
    Plays in the perfect garden of her martyrdom,
Ipsi soli servo fidem.

    Spending the silver of her little life
    To bring her Bridegroom these bright flowers
    Of which her arms are full.

Cujus pulchritudinem . . .
    With what white smiles
    She buys the Popes their palliums,
    And lavishes upon our souls the lambs of her con-
        fession!
Sol et luna mirantur,
Ipsi soli servo fidem.

Her virtues, with their simple strings,
Play to the Lover hidden in the universe,
Cujus pulchritudinem . . .

Who smiles into the sun His looking-glass,
And fills it with His glorious face:
Who utters the round moon's recurring O
And drowns our dusks in peace.
Ipsi soli servo fidem!

The Roman captain's work is done:
Now he may tear his temples down—
Her charity has flown to four horizons, like the
swiftest doves,

Where all towns sing like springtime, with their new-
born bells
Pouring her golden name out of their crucibles.

SONG

from Crossportion's Pastoral

The bottom of the sea has come
And builded in my noiseless room
The fishes' and the mermaids' home,

Whose it is most, most hell to be
Out of the heavy-hanging sea
And in the thin, thin changeable air

Or unroom sleep some other where;
But play their coral violins
Where waters most look music in:

The bottom of my room, the sea.
Full of voiceless curtaindeep
There mermaid somnambules come sleep
Where fluted half-lights show the way,

And there, there lost orchestras play
And down the many quarterlights come
To the dim mirth of my aquadrome:
The bottom of my sea, the room.

THE MAN IN THE WIND

Here is the man who fancies Arab ponies,
Captain April, walking like the wind,
Breeding the happy swordlight of the sun.

Secret, in his looks and manner,
He's not as inattentive to the music as he seems,
That jangles in the empty doorways.

But his well-tempered spirit,
Rapt in the middle of a harmony,
Flies to a breathless wedding with the Palisades.

Then his five senses, separate as their numbers,
Scatter, like birds, from in front of his steps,
And instantly return, like water,
To the common Bermuda of the flashing river.

The mathematics of the air describes a perfect silence,
And Captain April's mind, leaning out of its own
    amazing windows,
Dies in a swirl of doves.

ARIADNE

All through the blazing afternoon
The hand drums talk together like locusts;
The flute pours out its endless, thin stream,
Threading it in and out the clatter of sticks upon
    wood-blocks.
Drums and bells exchange handfuls of bright coins,
Drums and bells scatter their music, like pennies, all
    over the air,
And see, the lutanist's thin hand
Rapidly picks the spangling notes off from his wires
And throws them about like drops of water.

Behind the bamboo blinds,
Behind the palms,
In the green, sundappled apartments of her palace
Redslippered Ariadne, with a tiny yawn,
Tosses a ball upon her roulette wheel.

Suddenly, dead north,
A Greek ship leaps over the horizon, skips like a colt,
    paws the foam.
The ship courses through the pasture of bright ame-
    thysts
And whinnies at the jetty.
The whole city runs to see:
Quick as closing your hand
The racing sail's down.
Then the drums are stunned, and the crowd, exalted,
    cries:
O Theseus! O Grecian hero!

Like a thought through the mind
Ariadne moves to the window.
Arrows of light, in every direction,
Leap from the armor of the black-eyed captain.
Arrows of light
Resound within her like the strings of a guitar.

TROPICS

At noon the sky goes off like a gun.

Guards, on the Penal Island,
Converging, mad as murder, in the swearing cane,
Arrest the four-footed wind.

23

But the chained and numbered men
Do not cease their labor:
Building a cage for the devouring sun.

At six o'clock exactly,
The day explodes like a bomb,
And it is night.

Instantly, the guards
Hide in the jungle, build a boat
And escape.

But the prisoners of the state
Do not cease their labor:
Collecting the asphalt fragments of the night.

ASH WEDNESDAY

The naked traveller,
Stretching, against the iron dawn, the bowstrings of
    his eyes,
Starves on the mad sierra.

But the sleepers,
Prisoners in a lovely world of weeds,
Make a small, red cry,
And change their dreams.

24

Proud as the mane of the whinnying air,
Yet humble as the flakes of water
Or the chips of the stone sun, the traveller
Is nailed to the hill by the light of March's razor;

And when the desert barks, in a rage of love
For the noon of the eclipse,
He lies with his throat cut, in a frozen crater.

Then the sleepers,
Prisoners of a moonward power of tides,
Slain by the stillness of their own reflections,
Sit up, in their graves, with a white cry,
And die of terror at the traveller's murder.

CRUSOE

Sometimes the sun beats up the rocks of capes
And robs the green world with a clangor of banks.

Then the citizens
Come out to stone the sky; and with their guns
Mean to shoot the highpowered spheres to pieces:
At dawn, the laws, in the yards of all the prisons,
Propose to hang the robber, the breeder of life.

What if no more men will learn to turn again
And run to the rainy world's boundaries?
What if no more men will learn to atone

By hard, horseplay of shipwreck in the drench of Ma-
    gellan,
And still steer by the stars' unending Lent?

What if the last man
Will no more learn, and run
The stern, foundering ocean, north of the line,
Where crew and cargo drown in the thrash of the
    wreck,
The day he's driven to his Penal Island,
His own rich acre of island, like the wiseguy Crusoe!

APRIL

April, like a leopard in the windy woods,
Sports with the javelins of the weather;

And the hunters,
Eye-level with the world's clean brim,
Sight their strings, in masking rocks not moving,
And shower with arrows
The innocent, immortal season.

Hear how like lights these following releases
Of sharpened shaft-flights sing across the air,
And play right through, unwounding, clearest wind-
    works—

To disappear, unpublished, in the reeds.

But where their words are quenched, the world is
    quickened:
The lean air suddenly flowers,
The little voices of the rivers change;

So that the hunters put away their silver quivers,
Die to the level of river and rockbrim,
And are translated, homeward,
To the other, solemn, world.

THE GREEK WOMEN

The ladies in red capes and golden bracelets
Walk like reeds and talk like rivers,
And sigh, like Vichy water, in the doorways;

And looks run down the land like colts,
Race with the wind, (the mares, their mothers', lover)
Down to the empty harbor.

All spine and sandal stand the willow women;
They shake their silver bangles
In the olive-light of clouds and windows,
Talking, among themselves, like violins;

And, opening their eyes wide as horizons,
Seem to await the navy home from Troy.

No longer stand together, widow women!
Give your gold ornaments to the poor,
Make run the waterspeech of beads between your
     fingers:
For Troy is burned, and Greece is cursed,
The plague comes like a cloud.
All your men are sleeping in the alien earth,

But one.
And Clytemnestra, walking like a willow, stares.
Beads and bracelets gently knifeclash all about her,
Because the conqueror, the homecome hero,
The soldier, Agamemnon,
Bleeds in her conscience, twisting like a root.

CALYPSO'S ISLAND

See with how little motion, now, the noon wind
Fills the woods' eyes with flirting oleanders,
While perpendicular sun lets fall
Nickels and dimes on the deep harbor.

Fair cries of divers fly in the air
Amid the rigging of the newcome schooner,
And the white ship
Rides like a petal on the purple water
And flings her clangorous anchor in the quiet deeps,
And wrecks the waving waterlights.

Then Queen Calypso
Wakes from a dreaming lifetime in her house of
    wicker,
Sees all at once the shadows on the matting
Coming and going like a leopard;
Hears for the first time the flame-feathered birds
Shout their litany in the savage tree;

And slowly tastes the red red wound
Of the sweet pomegranate,

And lifts her eyelids like the lids of treasures.

THE OHIO RIVER—LOUISVILLE

No one can hear the loud voice of the city
Because of the tremendous silence
Of this slow-moving river, quiet as space.

Not the towering bridge, the crawling train,
Not the knives of pylons
Clashing in the sun,
And not the sky-swung cables;
Not the outboard boat
Swearing in the fiery distance like a locust,
Not the iron cries of men:
Nothing is heard,
Only the immense and silent movement of the river.

The trains go through the summer quiet as paper,
And, in the powerhouse, the singing dynamos
Make no more noise than cotton.
All life is quieter than the weeds
On which lies lightly sprawling,
Like white birds shot to death,
The bathers' clothing.

But only where the swimmers float like alligators,
And with their eyes as dark as creosote
Scrutinize the murderous heat,
Only there is anything heard:
The thin, salt voice of violence,
That whines, like a mosquito, in their simmering
    blood.

THE HOUSE OF CAIPHAS

Somewhere, inside the wintry colonnade,
Stands, like a churchdoor statue, God's Apostle,
Good St. Peter, by the brazier,
With his back turned to the trial.

As scared and violent as flocks of birds of prey,
The testimonies of the holy beggars
Fly from the stones, and scatter in the windy shadows.

The accusations of the holy judge
Rise, in succession, dignified as rockets,

Soar out of silence to their towering explosions
And, with their meteors, raid the earth.

And the gates of night fall shut with the clangor of
    arms.

The crafty eyes of witnesses, set free to riot,
Now shine as sharp as needles at the carved Apostle's
    mantle.
Voices begin to rise, like water, in the colonnade;
Fingers accuse him like a herd of cattle.

Then the Apostle, white as marble, weak as tin
Cries out upon the crowd:
And, no less artificial than the radios of his voice,
He flees into the freezing night.

And all the constellations vanish out of heaven
With a glassy cry;
Cocks crow as sharp as steel in the terrible, clear east,

And the gates of night fall shut with the thunder of
    Massbells.

AUBADE—HARLEM

(For Baroness C. de Hueck)

Across the cages of the keyless aviaries,
The lines and wires, the gallows of the broken kites,
Crucify; against the fearful light,
The ragged dresses of the little children.
Soon, in the sterile jungles of the waterpipes and
     ladders,
The bleeding sun, a bird of prey, will terrify the poor,
Who will forget the unbelievable moon.

But in the cells and wards of whiter buildings,
Where the glass dawn is brighter than the knives of
     surgeons,
Paler than alcohol or ether,
Greyer than guns and shinier than money,
The white men's wives, like Pilate's,
Cry in the peril of their frozen dreams:

"Daylight has driven iron spikes,
Into the flesh of Jesus' hands and feet:
Four flowers of blood have nailed Him to the walls
     of Harlem."

Along the white walls of the clinics and the hospitals
Pilate vanishes with a cry:
They have cut down two hundred Judases,
Hanged by the neck in the opera houses and mu-
     seums.

Across the cages of the keyless aviaries,
The lines and wires, the gallows of the broken kites,
Crucify, against the fearful light,
The ragged dresses of the little children.

DIRGE FOR A TOWN IN FRANCE

Up among the stucco pears, the iron vines,
Mute as their watered roses, their mimosas,
The wives gaze down among the traceries
Of balconies: the one-time finery
Of iron, suburban balconies.

Down in the shadowy doors,
Men fold their arms,
And hearken after the departing day
That somewhere sings more softly
Than merry-go-rounds in distant fairs.

O, it is not those first, faint stars
Whose fair light, falling, whispers in the river;
And it is not the dusty wind,
Waving the waterskirts of the shy-talking fountain,

That wakes the wooden horses' orchestra,
The fifing goldfinch, and the phony flute,
And the steam robins and electric nightingales
That blurred the ding of cymbals,

That other time, when childhood turned and turned
As grave as sculpture in a zodiac.

And yet the mystery comes on
Spontaneous as the street-lights, in the plane trees:
The trees, whose paint falls off in flakes,
Elaborate as the arches
Of a deserted opera!

The roses and mimosas in the windows
Adore the night they breathe, not understanding;
The women dream of bread and chocolate
In their aquariums
Of traceries, and lace, and cherubim;

But the men die, down in the shadowy doors,
The way their thoughts die in their eyes,
To see those sad and funny children
Run down the colonnade of trees
Where the carnival doesn't exist:

Those children, who are lost too soon,
With fading laughter, on the road along the river:
Gone, like the slowing cavalcade, the homeward
    horses.

AUBADE—THE CITY

Now that the clouds have come like cattle
To the cold waters of the city's river,
All the windows turn their scandalized expression
Toward the tide's tin dazzle,

And question, with their weak-eyed stare,
The riotous sun.

From several places at a time
Cries of defiance,
As delicate as frost, as sharp as glass,
Rise from the porcelain buildings
And break in the blue sky.

Then, falling swiftly from the air,
The fragments of this fragile indignation
Ring on the echoing streets
No louder than a shower of pins.

But suddenly the bridges' choiring cables
Jangle gently in the wind
And play like quiet piano-strings.

All down the faces of the buildings
Windows begin to close
Like figures in a long division.

Those whose eyes all night have simulated sleep,
Suddenly stare, from where they lie, like wolves,
Tied in the tangle of the bedding,

And listen for the waking blood
To flood the apprehensive silence of their flesh.
They fear the heart that now lies quenched may quicken,
And start to romp against the rib,
Soft and insistent as a secret bell.

They also fear the light will grow
Into the windows of their hiding places, like a tree
Of tropical flowers
And put them, one by one, to flight.

Then life will have to begin.
Pieces of paper, lying in the streets,
Will start up, in the twisting wind,
And fly like idiot birds before the faces of the crowds.
And in the roaring buildings
Elevator doors will have begun
To clash like sabres.

THE PERIL

When anger comes to the coast of our desolate country
And the sky is the color of armor,
We listen, in the silence of the cliffs and bays as still as
    steel,
For the cry that terrifies the sentinel.
And if it sound, oh! suddener than Java dancers
Face us all the swords we fear.
Well, we have arms: we will put them to trial.

But even as we wait, in hiding, for the unknown sig-
    nal,
It is the Bridegroom comes like lightning where we
    never looked!
His eyes are angels, armed in smiles of fire.
His Word puts out the spark of every other sun
Faster than sunlight ever hid the cities
Of the fire-crowded universe!
How shall I stand such light, being dim as my fear?

Rob me, and make me poor enough to bear my price-
    less ransom;
Lock me and dower me in the gifts and jails of tribu-
    lation:
Stab me and save me with the five lights of Your
    Crucifixion!

37

And I'll become as strong as wax, as weak as dia-
    monds,
And read Your speeches deeper than the sea
And, like the sky, fair!

ADVENT

Charm with your stainlessness these winter nights,
Skies, and be perfect!
Fly vivider in the fiery dark, you quiet meteors,
And disappear.
You moon, be slow to go down,
This is your full!

The four white roads make off in silence
Towards the four parts of the starry universe.
Time falls like manna at the corners of the wintry
    earth.
We have become more humble than the rocks,
More wakeful than the patient hills.

Charm with your stainlessness these nights in Advent,
    holy spheres,
While minds, as meek as beasts,
Stay close at home in the sweet hay;
And intellects are quieter than the flocks that feed by
    starlight.

Oh pour your darkness and your brightness over all
    our solemn valleys,
You skies: and travel like the gentle Virgin,
Toward the planets' stately setting,

Oh white full moon as quiet as Bethlehem!

CAROL

Flocks feed by darkness with a noise of whispers,
In the dry grass of pastures,
And lull the solemn night with their weak bells.

The little towns upon the rocky hills
Look down as meek as children:
Because they have seen come this holy time.

God's glory, now, is kindled gentler than low candle-
    light
Under the rafters of a barn:
Eternal Peace is sleeping in the hay,
And Wisdom's born in secret in a straw-roofed stable.

And O! Make holy music in the stars, you happy an-
    gels.
You shepherds, gather on the hill.
Look up, you timid flocks, where the three kings
Are coming through the wintry trees;

39

While we unnumbered children of the wicked cen-
 turies
Come after with our penances and prayers,
And lay them down in the sweet-smelling hay
Beside the wise men's golden jars.

THE CANDLEMAS PROCESSION

Lumen
Ad revelationem gentium.

Look kindly, Jesus, where we come,
New Simeons, to kindle,
Each at Your infant sacrifice his own life's candle.

And when Your flame turns into many tongues,
See how the One is multiplied, among us, hundreds!
And goes among the humble, and consoles our sinful
 kindred.

It is for this we come,
And, kneeling, each receive one flame:
Ad revelationem gentium.

Our lives, like candles, spell this simple symbol:

40

Weep like our bodily life, sweet work of bees,
Sweeten the world, with your slow sacrifice.
And this shall be our praise:
That by our glad expense, our Father's will
Burned and consumed us for a parable.

Nor burn we now with brown and smoky flames, but
        bright
Until our sacrifice is done,
(By which not we, but You are known)
And then, returning to our Father, one by one,
Give back our lives like wise and waxen lights.

CANA

"This beginning of miracles did Jesus
    in Cana of Galilee."

Once when our eyes were clean as noon, our rooms
Filled with the joys of Cana's feast:
For Jesus came, and His disciples, and His Mother,
And after them the singers
And some men with violins.

Once when our minds were Galilees,
And clean as skies our faces,
Our simple rooms were charmed with sun.

Our thoughts went in and out in whiter coats than
    God's disciples',
In Cana's crowded rooms, at Cana's tables.

Nor did we seem to fear the wine would fail:
For ready, in a row, to fill with water and a miracle,
We saw our earthen vessels, waiting empty.
What wine those humble waterjars foretell!

Wine for the ones who, bended to the dirty earth,
Have feared, since lovely Eden, the sun's fire,
Yet hardly mumble, in their dusty mouths, one prayer.

Wine for old Adam, digging in the briars!

ST. PAUL

When I was Saul, and sat among the cloaks,
My eyes were stones, I saw no sight of heaven,
Open to take the spirit of the twisting Stephen.
When I was Saul, and sat among the rocks,
I locked my eyes, and made my brain my tomb,
Sealed with what boulders rolled across my reason!

When I was Saul and walked upon the blazing desert
My road was quiet as a trap.
I feared what word would split high noon with light
And lock my life, and try to drive me mad:
And thus I saw the Voice that struck me dead.

Tie up my breath, and wind me in white sheets of
    anguish,
And lay me in my three days' sepulchre
Until I find my Easter in a vision.

Oh Christ! Give back my life, go, cross Damascus,
Find out my Ananias in that other room:
Command him, as you do, in this my dream;
He knows my locks, and owns my ransom,
Waits for Your word to take his keys and come.

TRAPPISTS, WORKING

Now all our saws sing holy sonnets in this world of
    timber
Where oaks go off like guns, and fall like cataracts,
Pouring their roar into the wood's green well.

Walk to us, Jesus, through the wall of trees,
And find us still adorers in these airy churches,
Singing our other Office with our saws and axes.
Still teach Your children in the busy forest,
And let some little sunlight reach us, in our mental
    shades, and leafy studies.

When time has turned the country white with grain
And filled our regions with the thrashing sun,
Walk to us, Jesus, through the walls of wheat

43

When our two tractors come to cut them down:
Sow some light winds upon the acres of our spirit,
And cool the regions where our prayers are reapers,
And slake us, Heaven, with Your living rivers.

ST. ALBERIC

When your loud axe's echo on the ponds, at early
    morning,
Scared the shy mallard from the shallows grey as tin,
The glades gave back your hammers' antiphons—
The din of nails that shamed the lazy spring.
Striving, like Adam, with the barren wildwood,
And with the desolation of the brake,
You builded, in a reedy place
A cloister and a Ladychurch.

But when the stones and clean-hewn beams
Heard no more sounds but of the bees, your thought-
    ful eyes
Were always full of exile,
Though peaceful with the peace of pilgrims, and with
    happiness
That shamed, in the deep wood, the sentimental doves.

When in the church your canticles were done,
Even your silences were better than the birds, whose
    song

44

Still fell, like fountains, from the forest to your sunny
    cloister.
And when, in the high-noon of contemplation, reason
    died by blindness,
Your faith escaped, and found the flowering Cross—
Loving, in Christ, the agony of Adam:
Body and Spirit tilled and gardened with our penances
    and death.

And from the flowers of that frightful Paradise,
(The wounds that heal the loving mind)
Your diligence could draw such excellence
As shamed the bees at work in the wild rock.

Then did you fill the cloisters of your intellect,
The tabernacles in the secret churches of your will.
Slowly you built sweet counsel, like a honeycomb,
And fed your life with living Wisdom, Heaven's es-
    sence.

THE BIOGRAPHY

Oh read the verses of the loaded scourges,
And what is written in their terrible remarks:
"The Blood runs down the walls of Cambridge town,
As useless as the waters of the narrow river—
While pub and alley gamble for His vesture."

45

Although my life is written on Christ's Body like a
  map,
The nails have printed in those open hands
More than the abstract names of sins,
More than the countries and the towns,
The names of streets, the numbers of the houses,
The record of the days and nights,
When I have murdered Him in every square and
  street.

Lance and thorn, and scourge and nail
Have more than made His Flesh my chronicle.
My journeys more than bite His bleeding feet.

Christ, from my cradle, I had known You everywhere,
And even though I sinned, I walked in You, and knew
    You were my world:
You were my France and England,
My seas and my America:
You were my life and air, and yet I would not own
    You.

Oh, when I loved You, even while I hated You,
Loving and yet refusing You in all the glories of Your
  universe

It was Your living Flesh I tore and trampled, not the
    air and earth:
Not that You feel us, in created things,
But knowing You, in them, made every sin a sacrilege;

46

And every act of greed became a desecration,
Spoiled and dishonored You as in Your Eucharist.

And yet with every wound You robbed me of a crime,
And as each blow was paid with Blood,
You paid me also each great sin with greater graces.
For even as I killed You,
You made Yourself a greater thief than any in Your
    company,
Stealing my sins into Your dying life,
Robbing me even of my death.

Where, on what cross my agony will come
I do not ask You:
For it is written and accomplished here,
On every Crucifix, on every altar.
It is my narrative that drowns and is forgotten
In Your five open Jordans,
Your voice that cries my: *"Consummatum est."*

If on Your Cross Your life and death and mine are
    one,
Love teaches me to read, in You, the rest of a new
    history.
I trace my days back to another childhood,
Exchanging, as I go,
New York and Cuba for Your Galilee,
And Cambridge for Your Nazareth,
Until I come again to my beginning,
And find a manger, star and straw,

A pair of animals, some simple men,
And thus I learn that I was born,
Now not in France, but Bethlehem.

AFTER THE NIGHT OFFICE—
GETHSEMANI ABBEY

It is not yet the grey and frosty time
When barns ride out of the night like ships:
We do not see the Brothers, bearing lanterns,
Sink in the quiet mist,
As various as the spirits who, with lamps, are sent
To search our souls' Jerusalems
Until our houses are at rest
And minds enfold the Word, our Guest.

Praises and canticles anticipate
Each day the singing bells that wake the sun,
But now our psalmody is done.
Our hasting souls outstrip the day:
Now, before dawn, they have their noon.
The Truth that transsubstantiates the body's night
Has made our minds His temple-tent:
Open the secret eye of faith
And drink these deeps of invisible light.

The weak walls
Of the world fall
And heaven, in floods, comes pouring in:

Sink from your shallows, soul, into eternity,
And slake your wonder at that deep-lake spring.
We touch the rays we cannot see,
We feel the light that seems to sing.

Go back to bed, red sun, you are too late,
And hide behind Mount Olivet—
For like the flying moon, held prisoner,
Within the branches of a juniper,
So in the cages of our consciousness
The Dove of God is prisoner yet:
Unruly sun, go back to bed.

But now the lances of the morning
Fire all their gold against the steeple and the water-
    tower.
Returning to the windows of our deep abode of peace,
Emerging at our conscious doors
We find our souls all soaked in grace, like Gedeon's
    fleece.

THE TRAPPIST CEMETERY—
GETHSEMANI

Brothers, the curving grasses and their daughters
Will never print your praises:
The trees our sisters, in their summer dresses,

Guard your fame in these green cradles:
The simple crosses are content to hide your characters.

Oh do not fear
The birds that bicker in the lonely belfry
Will ever give away your legends.
Yet when the sun, exulting like a dying martyr,
Canonizes, with his splendid fire, the sombre hills,
Your graves all smile like little children,
And your wise crosses trust the mothering night
That folds them in the Sanctuary's wings.

You need not hear the momentary rumors of the road
Where cities pass and vanish in a single car
Filling the cut beside the mill
With roar and radio,
Hurling the air into the wayside branches
Leaving the leaves alive with panic.

See, the kind universe,
Wheeling in love about the abbey steeple,
Lights up your sleepy nursery with stars.

* * *

God, in your bodily life,
Untied the snares of anger and desire,
Hid your flesh from envy by these country altars,
Beneath these holy eaves where even sparrows have
    their houses.
But oh, how like the swallows and the chimney swifts
Do your free souls in glory play!
And with a cleaner flight,

50

Keener, more graceful circles,
Rarer and finer arcs
Than all these innocent attacks that skim our steeple!
How like these children of the summer evening
Do your rejoicing spirits
Deride the dry earth with their aviation!

But now the treble harps of night begin to play in the
    deep wood,
To praise your holy sleep,
And all the frogs along the creek
Chant in the moony waters to the Queen of Peace.
And we, the mariners, and travellers,
The wide-eyed immigrants,
Praying and sweating in our steerage cabins,
Lie still and count with love the measured bells
That tell the deep-sea leagues until your harbor.

Already on this working earth you knew what name-
    less love
Adorns the heart with peace by night,
Hearing, adoring all the dark arrivals of eternity.
Oh, here on earth you knew what secret thirst
Arming the mind with instinct,
Answers the challenges of God with garrisons
Of unified desire
And facing Him in His new wars
Is slain at last in an exchange of lives.

Teach us, Cistercian Fathers, how to wear
Silence, our humble armor.
Pray us a torrent of the seven spirits

That are our wine and stamina:
Because your work is not yet done.
But look: the valleys shine with promises,
And every burning morning is a prophecy of Christ
Coming to raise and vindicate
Even our sorry flesh.

Then will your graves, Gethsemani, give up their
    angels,
Return them to their souls to learn
The songs and attitudes of glory.
Then will creation rise again like gold
Clean, from the furnace of your litanies:
The beasts and trees shall share your resurrection,
And a new world be born from these green tombs.

LA SALETTE

It is a hundred years since your shy feet
Ventured to stand upon the pasture grass of the high
    Alps,
Coming no deeper in our smoky atmosphere
Than these blue skies, the mountain eyes
Of the two shepherd children, young as flowers,
Born to be dazzled by no mortal snow.

Lady, it is a hundred years
Since those fair, terrible tears
Reproved, with their amazing grief

52

All the proud candor of those altitudes:
Crowning the flowers at your feet
With diamonds, that seized upon, transfigured into
    nails of light
The rays of the mountain sun!—

And by their news,
(Which came with cowbells to the evening village
And to the world with church-bells
After not too many days,)
And by their news

We thought the walls of all hard hearts
Had broken down, and given in,
Poured out their dirty garrisons of sin,
And washed the streets with our own blood, if need
    be—
—Only to have them clean!

And though we did not understand
The weight and import of so great a sorrow,
We never thought so soon to have seen
The loss of its undying memory,
Passing from the black world without a word,
Without a funeral!
For while our teeth were battling in the meat of mir-
    acles and favors,
Your words, your prophecies, were all forgotten!

Now, one by one,
The things you said
Have come to be fulfilled.

53

John, in the might of his Apocalypse, could not fore-
tell
Half of the story of our monstrous century,
In which the arm of your inexorable Son,
Bound, by His Truth, to disavow your intercession
For this wolf-world, this craven zoo,
Has bombed the doors of hell clean off their hinges,
And burst the cage of antichrist,
And roused, with His first two great thunderbolts,
The chariots of Armageddon.

LANDSCAPE, PROPHET AND WILD-DOG

The trees stand like figures in a theatre.
Then suddenly there comes a prophet, running for his
life,
And the wild-dog behind him.
And now the wild-dog has him by the ankle
And the man goes down.

"Oh prophet, when it was afternoon you told us:
'Tonight is the millenium,
The withering-away of the state.
The skies, in smiles, shall fold upon the world,
Melting all injustice in the rigors of their breezy
love.'
And all night long we waited at the desert's edge,
Hearing this wild-dog, only, on the far mountain,
Watching the white moon giggle in the stream!"

54

The two trees stand like Masters of Arts
And observe the wild-dog
Nailing his knives into the prophet's shoulder.

    "Oh prophet, when it was night you came and
        told us:
    'Tomorrow is the mellenium,
    The golden age!
    The human race will wake up
    And find dollars growing out of the palms of their
        hands,
    And the whole world will die of brotherly love
    Because the factories jig like drums
    And furnaces feed themselves,
    And all men lie in idleness upon the quilted pas-
        tures,
    Tuning their friendly radios and dreaming in the
        sun!"

    "But when the grey day dawned
    What flame flared in the jaws of the avenging
        mills!
    We heard the clash of hell within the gates of the
        embattled Factory
    And thousands died in the teeth of those sarcastic
        fires!"

    "And now the rivers are poisoned,
    The skies rain blood
    And all the springs are brackish with the taste
    Of these your prophecies.

55

Oh prophet, tell us plainly, at last:
When is the day of our success?"

But there is no answer in the dead jaws.
And the air is full of wings.
The crows come down and sit like senators
On the arms of the two trees.

At the edge of the salt-lands
In the dry-blue clay
The wild-dog, with a red claw scuffs out a little hol-
      low,
Burying the prophet's meatless shin.

LANDSCAPE: BEAST

Yonder, by the eastward sea
Where smoke melts in a saucer of extinguished cities,
The last men stand, in delegations,
Waiting to see the seven-headed business
Promised us, from those unpublished deeps:
Waiting to see those horns and diadems
And hear the seven voices of the final blasphemy.

And westward, where the other waters are as slick as
      silk
And slide, in the grey evening, with uncertain lights,
(Screened by the smoke of the extinguished studios)

56

The last men wait to see the seven-headed thing.
They stand around the radios
Wearing their regalia on their thin excited breasts,
Waving the signals of their masonry.
What will happen, when they see those heads, those
    horns
Dishevel the flickering sea?

How will they bare their foreheads, and put forth
    their hands
And wince with the last indelible brand,
And wear the dolour of that animal's number,
And evermore be burned with her disgusting name?

Inland, in the lazy distance, where a dozen planes still
    play
As loud as horseflies, round the ruins of an average
    town,
A blue-green medium dragon, swimming in the river,
Emerges from the muddy waters, comes to romp
    awhile upon the land.
She rises on the pathless shore,
And goes to roll in the ashes of the ravaged country.
But no man turns to see and be surprised
Where those grey flanks flash palely in the sun.
Who shall gather to see an ordinary dragon, in this
    day of anger,
Or wonder at those scales as usual as sin?

Meanwhile, upon the broken mountains of the south
No one observes the angels passing to and fro:

And no one sees the fire that shoots beneath the hoofs
Of all the white, impatient horses.

And no one hears or fears the music of those blazing
    swords.

(Northward, northward, what lies there to see?
Who shall recount the terror of those ruined streets?

And who shall dare to look where all the birds with
    golden beaks
Stab at the blue eyes of the murdered saints?)

THE HEAVENLY CITY

City, when we see you coming down,
Coming down from God
To be the new world's crown:
How shall they sing, the fresh, unsalted seas
Hearing your harmonies!

For there is no more death,
No need to cure those waters, now, with any brine;
Their shores give them no dead,
Rivers no blood, no rot to stain them.

Because the cruel algebra of war
Is now no more.
And the steel circle of time, inexorable,

Bites like a padlock shut, forever,
In the smoke of the last bomb:
And in that trap the murderers and sorcerers and
    crooked leaders
Go rolling home to hell.
And history is done.

Shine with your lamb-light, shine upon the world:
You are the new creation's sun.
And standing on their twelve foundations,
Lo, the twelve gates that are One Christ are wide as
    canticles:
And Oh! Begin to hear the thunder of the songs
    within the crystal Towers,
While all the saints rise from their earth with feet like
    light
And fly to tread the quick-gold of those streets,

Oh, City, when we see you sailing down,
Sailing down from God,
Dressed in the glory of the Trinity, and angel-
    crowned
In nine white diadems of liturgy.

THREE POSTCARDS FROM THE MONASTERY

I

The pilgrim passes swiftly.
All the strange towns,
Wrapped in their double cloaks
(Of rain and of non-entity)
Veil their elusive faces.

The pale world, white as plaster,
(Its doors are dumb, its windows far too blind for
    lamentation)
Dies like problematical news.

We have receded from the things
You printed on those unidentified façades.
We barely dream about the frontispiece
Of your collapsing palaces.
We can refuse your tin.

The smoky choirs
Of those far five-o'clock trombones
Have blown away. Our eyes
Are clean as the September night.
Our minds, (our silences) are light years deep.

Who shall amaze us with the noise of your discovery,
    America?
Who shall make known to us your new, true name,
Instead of knocking at our gates,
Bidding us look again upon that blank and pictured
    concentration?

Because the ticker-tapes are dead,
The radios are all shot:
But we have gone up to buy you Andromeda.

II

It is because the sun
Shines on the shallows like a cannonade
That we have come inland.

It is because the cloudy sea
Hailing the cliffs as loud as promises,
Saluting all the continent with foaming orchestras,

Raided the shore with tons of silver
That we have fled to the penniless hills,
Hidden in the poor, laborious fields.

We stood one moment by the bridgehead of those fatal
    fortunes:
Days that offered to fill our hands with gold,
Surfs that crowded the grey rocks with ballyhoo.

61

Shall I speak plain against the sun?
Or sing together with the comic-operas of the sea?
We have refused the reward,
We have abandoned the man-hunt.
But when the contest is over
We shall inherit the world.

III

Once were begotten
In the wombs of the deep mountains:
Born over and over in the play of penitential tunnels.
Such was our birth and resurrection from the freezing
    east
The night we cleared you, Pittsburgh, in a maze of
    lights.

Our lives were suddenly weaned in strange Ohio,
(Whose towns made little love to us, in their green
    requiems)
Weaned from the land and atmosphere of men.

Have you ever heard this music
Sung over and over by night,
How we will live *in loco pascuae*?
Or the assuring voices of those inward violins
Play: "Going to Gethsemani?"

(We were begotten in the tunnels of December rain,
Born from the wombs of news and tribulation.
By night, by wakeful rosary:

Such was my birth, my resurrection from the freezing
  east,
The night we cleared you, Cincinnati, in a maze of
  lights.)

ON THE ANNIVERSARY OF MY BAPTISM

Certain waters are as blue as metal
Or as salt as sorrow.
Others wince like brass in the hammering sun,
Or stammer all over with tremors of shadow
That die as fast as the light winds
Whose flights surprise the promontories
And the marble bay.

Some are crowded everywhere, off-shore, with purple
  coral
Between the fleets of light that founder in the sand.
Others are full of yawls, or loud with launches,
Or sadder than the bitter smoke
Of tug and trawler, tramp and collier,

Or as grey as battle.

Oh! Since I was a baby in the Pyrenees,
When old St. Martin marked me for the cloister from
  high Canigou,

63

How many deeps, how many wicked seas
Went to befriend me with a flash of white-caps
Louder than laughter in the wind and sun,
Or sluggered all our brown bows gunwale-under
In their rowdy thunder—
Only to return me to the land.

Do you suppose that if the green Atlantic
Had ever cracked our brittle shell
And rifled all the cabins for their fruit of drunken
      passengers,
Do you suppose my sins,
Once we were sorted and disposed forever
Along the shelves of that profound, unvisited mu-
      seum,
Would there have been immune,
Or learned to keep their coats of unreality
From the deep sea's most patient candying?

The day You made the waters,
And dragged them down from the dividing islands
And made them spring with fish,
You planned to bless the brine out of the seas
That were to be my death.

And this is the ninth November since my world's end
      and my Genesis,
When, with the sting of salt in my dry mouth,
Cross-crowned with water by the priest,
Stunned at the execution of my old companion, death,

And with the murder of my savage history,
You drowned me in the shallow font.

My eyes, swimming in unexpected infancy,
Were far too frail for such a favor:
They still close-kept the stone shell of their empty
    sepulchre:
But, though they saw none, guessed the new-come
    Trinity
That charged my sinews with His secret life.

DUNS SCOTUS

Striking like lightning to the quick of the real world
Scotus has mined all ranges to their deepest veins:
But where, oh, on what blazing mountain of theology
And in what Sinai's furnace
Did God refine that gold?

Who ruled those arguments in their triumphant order
And armed them with their strict celestial light?
See the lance-lightning, blade-glitter, banner-progress
As love advances, company by company
In sunlit teams his clean embattled reasons,

Until the firmament, with high heavenly marvel
Views in our crystal souls her blue embodiment,
Unfurls a thousand flags above our heads—
It is the music of Our Lady's army!

65

For Scotus is her theologian,
Nor has there ever been a braver chivalry than his
    precision.
His thoughts are skies of cloudless peace
Bright as the vesture of her grand aurora
Filled with the rising Christ.

But we, a weak, suspicious generation,
Loving emotion, hating prayer,
We are not worthy of his wisdom.
Creeping like beasts between the mountain's feet
We look for laws in the Arabian dust.
We have no notion of his freedom

Whose acts despise the chains of choice and passion.
We have no love for his beatitude
Whose act renounces motion:
Whose love flies home forever
As silver as felicity,
Working and quiet in the dancelight of an everlasting
    arrow.

Lady, the image of whose heaven
Sings in the might of Scotus' reasoning:
There is no line of his that has not blazed your glory
    in the schools,
Though in dark words, without romance,
Calling us to swear you our liege.

Language was far too puny for his great theology:
But, oh! His thought strode through those words

66

Bright as the conquering Christ
Between the clouds His enemies:
And in the clearing storm and Sinai's dying thunder
Scotus comes out, and shakes his golden locks
And sings like the African sun.

EVENING: ZERO WEATHER

Now the lone world is streaky as a wall of marble
With veins of clear and frozen snow.
There is no bird-song there, no hare's track
No badger working in the russet grass:
All the bare fields are silent as eternity.

And the whole herd is home in the long barn.
The brothers come, with hoods about their faces,
Following their plumes of breath
Lugging the gleaming buckets one by one.

This was a day when shovels would have struck
Full flakes of fire out of the land like rock:
And ground cries out like iron beneath our boots

When all the monks come in with eyes as clean as the
    cold sky
And axes under their arms,
Still paying out *Ave Marias*
With rosaries between their bleeding fingers.

We shake the chips out of our robes outside the door
And go to hide in cowls as deep as clouds,
Bowing our shoulders in the church's shadow, lean
and whipped,
To wait upon your Vespers, Mother of God!

And we have eyes no more for the dark pillars or the
freezing windows,
Ears for the rumorous cloister or the chimes of time
above our heads:
For we are sunken in the summer of our adoration,
And plunge, down, down into the fathoms of our
secret joy
That swims with indefinable fire.

And we will never see the copper sunset
Linger a moment, like an echo, on the frozen hill
Then suddenly die an hour before the Angelus.

For we have found our Christ, our August
Here in the zero days before Lent—
We are already binding up our sheaves of harvest
Beating the lazy liturgy, going up with exultation
Even on the eve of our Ash Wednesday,
And entering our blazing heaven by the doors of the
Assumption!

FREEDOM AS EXPERIENCE

When, as the captive of Your own invincible consent,
You love the image of Your endless Love,
Three-Personed God, what intellect
Shall take the measure of that liberty?

Compared with Love, Your Triune Law,
All the inexorable stars are anarchists:
Yet they are bound by Love and Love is infinitely free.

Minds cannot understand, nor systems imitate
The scope of such simplicity.
All the desires and hungers that defy Your Law
Wither to fears, and perish in imprisonment:
And all the hopes that seem to founder in the shadows
    of a cross
Wake from a momentary sepulchre, and they are
    blinded by their freedom!

Because our natures poise and point towards You
Our loves revolve about You as the planets swing
    upon the sun
And all suns sing together in their gravitational
    worlds.

And so, some days in prayer Your Love,
Prisoning us in darkness from the values of Your
    universe,

Delivers us from measure and from time,
Melts all the barriers that stop our passage to eternity
And solves the hours our chains.

And then, as fires like jewels germinate
Deep in the stone heart of a Kaffir mountain,
So now our gravity, our new-created deep desire
Burns in our life's mine like an undiscovered diamond.

Locked in that strength we stay and stay
And cannot go away
For You have given us our liberty.

Imprisoned in the fortunes of Your adamant
We can no longer move, for we are free.

THE SOWING OF MEANINGS

See the high birds! Is their's the song
That flies among the wood-light
Wounding the listener with such bright arrows?
Or do they play in wheeling silences
Defining in the perfect sky
The bounds of (here below) our solitude,

Where spring has generated lights of green
To glow in clouds upon the sombre branches?

Ponds full of sky and stillnesses
What heavy summer songs still sleep
Under the tawny rushes at your brim?

More than a season will be born here, nature,
In your world of gravid mirrors!
The quiet air awaits one note,
One light, one ray and it will be the angels' spring:
One flash, one glance upon the shiny pond, and then
Asperges me! sweet wilderness, and lo! we are re-
    deemed!

For, like a grain of fire
Smouldering in the heart of every living essence
God plants His undivided power——
Buries His thought too vast for worlds
In seed and root and blade and flower,

Until, in the amazing light of April,
Surcharging the religious silence of the spring,
Creation finds the pressure of His everlasting secret
Too terrible to bear.

Then every way we look, lo! rocks and trees
Pastures and hills and streams and birds and firma-
    ment
And our own souls within us flash, and shower us
    with light,
While the wild countryside, unknown, unvisited of
    men,
Bears sheaves of clean, transforming fire.

71

And then, oh then the written image, schooled in
    sacrifice,
The deep united threeness printed in our being,
Shot by the brilliant syllable of such an intuition,
    turns within,
And plants that light far down into the heart of dark-
    ness and oblivion,
Dives after, and discovers flame.

THE LANDFALL

We are beyond the ways of the far ships
Here in this coral port,
Farther than the ways of fliers,
Because our destinies have suddenly transported us
Beyond the brim of the enamel world.

O Mariner, what is the name of this uncharted Land?
On these clean shores shall stand what sinless voyager,
What angel breathe the music of this atmosphere?

Look where the thin flamingoes
Burning upon the purple shallows with their rare,
    pale flames,
Stand silent as our thought, although the birds in the
    high rock
Rinse our new senses with no mortal note,
What are these wings whose silks amaze the traveller?

The flowering palms charm all the strand
With their supernal scent.
The oleander and the wild hibiscus paint
The land with blood, and unknown blooms
Open to us the Gospel of their five wild wounds.

And the deep ferns sing this epithalame:
"Go up, go up! this desert is the door of heaven!
And it shall prove your frail soul's miracle!
Climb the safe mountain,

Disarm your labored flesh, and taste the treasure of
        these silences
In the high coral hermitage,
While the clean winds bemuse you in the clefted rock;
Or find you there some leafy Crusoe-castle: dwell in
        trees!

Take down the flagons of the blue and crimson fruits
And reap the everlasting wheat that no man's hand
        has sown,
And strike the rock that runs with waters strong as
        wine
To fill you with their fortitude:
Because this island is your Christ, your might, your
        fort, your paradise.

And lo! dumb time's grey, smoky argosies
Will never anchor in this emerald harbor
Or find this world of amber,
Spoil the fair music of the silver sea

Or foul these chiming amethysts:
Nor comes there any serpent near this isle trenched
    in deep ocean
And walled with innocent, flowering vines.

But from beyond the cotton clouds,
Between those lovely, white cathedrals full of sun,
The angels study beauty with their steps
And tread like notes of music down the beamy air
To gain this new world's virgin shore:
While from the ocean's jeweled floor
The long-lost divers, rising one by one,
Smile and throw down their dripping fortunes on the
    sand,
And sing us the strange tale
Of the drowned king (our nature), his return!

THE READER

Lord, when the clock strikes
Telling the time with cold tin
And I sit hooded in this lectern

Waiting for the monks to come,
I see the red cheeses, and bowls
All smile with milk in ranks upon their tables.

Light fills my proper globe
(I have won light to read by
With a little, tinkling chain)

And the monks come down the cloister
With robes as voluble as water.
I do not see them but I hear their waves.

It is winter, and my hands prepare
To turn the pages of the saints:
And to the trees Thy moon has frozen on the windows
My tongue shall sing Thy Scripture.

Then the monks pause upon the step
(With me here in this lectern
And Thee there on Thy crucifix)
And gather little pearls of water on their fingers' ends
Smaller than this my psalm.

ST. MALACHY

In November, in the days to remember the dead
When air smells cold as earth,
St. Malachy, who is very old, gets up,
Parts the thin curtains of trees and dawns upon our
    land.

His coat is filled with drops of rain, and he is bearded
With all the seas of Poseidon.

75

(Is it a crozier, or a trident in his hand?)
He weeps against the gothic window, and the empty
    cloister
Mourns like an ocean shell.

Two bells in the steeple
Talk faintly to the old stranger
And the tower considers his waters.
"I have been sent to see my festival," (his cavern
    speaks!)
"For I am the saint of the day.
Shall I shake the drops from my locks and stand in
    your transept,
Or, leaving you, rest in the silence of my history?"

So the bells rang and we opened the antiphoners
And the wrens and larks flew up out of the pages.
Our thoughts became lambs. Our hearts swam like
    seas.
One monk believed that we should sing to him
Some stone-age hymn
Or something in the giant language.
So we played to him in the plainsong of the giant
    Gregory:
Oceans of Scripture sang upon bony Eire.

Then the last salvage of flowers
(Fostered under glass after the gardens foundered)
Held up their little lamps on Malachy's altar
To peer into his wooden eyes before the Mass began.

Rain sighed down the sides of the stone church.
Storms sailed by all day in battle fleets.

At five o'clock, when we tried to see the sun, the
    speechless visitor
Sighed and arose and shook the humus from his feet
And with his trident stirred our trees
And left down-wood, shaking some drops upon the
    ground.

Thus copper flames fall, tongues of fire fall
The leaves in hundreds fall upon his passing
While night sends down her dreadnought darkness
Upon this spurious Pentecost.

And the Melchisedec of our year's end
Who came without a parent, leaves without a trace,
And rain comes rattling down upon our forest
Like the doors of a country jail.

THE CAPTIVES—A PSALM

*Quomodo cantabimus canticum Domini in terra
aliena?*

Somewhere a king walks in his gallery
Owning the gorges of a fiery city.
Brass traffic shakes the walls. The windows shiver
    with business.
It is the bulls' day. The citizens
Build themselves each hour another god
And fry a fatter idol out of mud.

77

They cut themselves a crooked idiom
To the winged animals, upon their houses.
Prayers are made of money, songs of numbers,
Hymns of the blood of the killed.

Old ladies are treasured in sugar.
Young ones rot in wine.
The flesh of the fat organizers smiles with oil.

Blessed is the army that will one day crush you, city,
Like a golden spider.
Blest are they that hate you. Blest are they
That dash your brats against the stones.

The children of God have died, O Babylon,
Of thy wild algebra.

Days, days are the journey
From wall to wall. And miles
Miles of houses shelter terror.
And we lie chained to their dry roots, O Israel!

Our bodies are greyer than mud.
There, butterflies are born to be dancers
And fly in black and blue along the drunken river
Where, in the willow trees, Assyria lynched our song!

May my bones burn and ravens eat my flesh
If I forget thee, contemplation!
May language perish from my tongue
If I do not remember thee, O Sion, city of vision,

Whose heights have windows finer than the firma-
ment
When night pours down her canticles
And peace sings on thy watchtowers like the stars of
Job.

IN THE RAIN AND THE SUN

Watch out for this peeled doorlight!
Here, without rain, without shame
My noonday dusk made spots upon the walk:
Tall drops pelted the concrete with their jewelry
Belonging to the old world's bones.

Owning this view, in the air of a hermit's weather,
I count the fragmentary rain
In drops as blue as coal
Until I plumb the shadows full of thunder.
My prayers supervise the atmosphere
Till storms call all hounds home.

Out of the towers of water
Four or five mountains come walking
To see the little monks' graves.
Flying the neutral stones I dwell between cedars
And see the countries sleeping in their beds:
Lands of the watermen, where poplars bend.

Wild seas amuse the world with water:
No end to all the surfs that charm our shores
Fattening the sands with their old foam and their old
    roar.

Thus in the boom of waves' advantage
Dogs and lions come to my tame home
Won by the bells of my Cistercian jungle.
O love the livid fringes
In which their robes are drenched!

Songs of the lions and whales!
With my pen between my fingers
Making the waterworld sing!
Sweet Christ, discover diamonds
And sapphires in my verse
While I burn the sap of my pine house
For praise of the ocean sun.

I have walked upon the whole days' surf
Rinsing Thy bays with hymns.
My eyes have swept horizons clean
Of ships and rain.
Upon the lacquered swells my feet no longer run.
Sliding all over the sea I come
To the hap of a slippery harbor.

Dogs have gone back to their ghosts
And the many lions, home.

But words fling wide the windows of their houses—
Adam and Eve walk down my coast
Praising the tears of the treasurer sun:

I hang Thy rubies on these autumn trees,
On the bones of the homegoing thunder.

DRY PLACES

No cars go by
Where dogs are barking at the desert.
Yet it is not twenty years since many lamps
Shed their juices in this one time town
And stores grew big lights, like oranges and pears.

Now not one lame miner
Sits on the rotten verandah,
Works in the irons where
Judas' shadow dwells.
Yet I could hew a city
From the side of their hill.

O deep stone covert where the dusk
Is full of lighted beasts
And the mad stars preach wars without end:
Whose bushes and grasses live without water,

There the skinny father of hate rolls in his dust
And if the wind should shift one leaf
The dead jump up and bark for their ghosts:
Their dry bones want our penniless souls.

Bones, go back to your baskets.
Get your fingers out of my clean skin.
Rest in your rainless death until your own souls
Come back in the appointed way and sort you out
    from your remains.

We who are still alive will wring a few green blades
From the floor of this valley
Though ploughs abhor your metal and your clay.
Rather than starve with you in rocks without oasis,

We will get up and work your loam
Until some prayer or some lean sentence
Bleeds like the quickest root they ever cut.

For we cannot forget the legend of the world's child-
    hood
Or the track to the dogwood valley
And Adam our Father's old grass farm
Wherein they gave the animals names
And knew Christ was promised first without scars
When all God's larks called out to Him
In their wild orchard.

A RESPONSORY, 1948

Suppose the dead could crown their wit
With some intemperate exercise,
Spring wine from their ivory
Or roses from their eyes?

Or if the wise could understand
And the world without heart
That the dead are not yet dead
And that the living live apart

And the wounded are healing,
Though in a place of flame.
The sick in a great ship
Are riding. They are riding home.

Suppose the dead could crown their wit
With some intemperate exercise,
Spring wine from their ivory
Or roses from their eyes?

Two cities sailed together
For many thousand years.
And now they drift asunder.
The tides of new wars

Sweep the sad heavens,
Divide the massed stars,
The black and white universe
The blooming spheres.

Down, down, down
The white armies fall
Moving their ordered snows
Toward the jaws of hell.

Suppose the dead could crown their wit
With some intemperate exercise,
Spring wine from their ivory
Or roses from their eyes?

A PSALM

When psalms surprise me with their music
And antiphons turn to rum
The Spirit sings: the bottom drops out of my soul

And from the center of my cellar, Love, louder than
    thunder
Opens a heaven of naked air.

New eyes awaken.
I send Love's name into the world with wings
And songs grow up around me like a jungle.
Choirs of all creatures sing the tunes
Your Spirit played in Eden.
Zebras and antelopes and birds of paradise
Shine on the face of the abyss
And I am drunk with the great wilderness
Of the sixth day in Genesis.

84

But sound is never half so fair
As when that music turns to air
And the universe dies of excellence.

Sun, moon and stars
Fall from their heavenly towers.
Joys walk no longer down the blue world's shore.

Though fires loiter, lights still fly on the air of the
    gulf,
All fear another wind, another thunder:
Then one more voice
Snuffs all their flares in one gust.

And I go forth with no more wine and no more stars
And no more buds and no more Eden
And no more animals and no more sea:

While God sings by himself in acres of night
And walls fall down, that guarded Paradise.

SENESCENTE MUNDO

Senescente mundo, when the hot globe
Shrivels and cracks
And uninhibited atoms resolve
Earth and water, fruit and flower, body and animal
    soul,
All the blue stars come tumbling down.

Beauty and ugliness and love and hate
Wisdom and politics are all alike undone.

Toward that fiery day we run like crabs
With our bad-tempered armor on.
"With blood and carpets, oranges and ashes,
Rubber and limes and bones,"
(So sing the children on the Avenue)
"With cardboard and dirty water and a few flames for
        the Peacelover's ghost,
We know where the dead bodies are
Studying the ceiling from the floors of their homes,
With smoke and roses, slate and wire
And crushed fruit and much fire."

Yet in the middle of this murderous season
Great Christ, my fingers touch Thy wheat
And hold Thee hidden in the compass of Thy paper
        sun.
There is no war will not obey this cup of Blood,
This wine in which I sink Thy words, in the anony-
        mous dawn!
I hear a Sovereign talking in my arteries
Reversing, with His Promises, all things
That now go on with fire and thunder.
His Truth is greater than disaster.
His Peace imposes silence on the evidence against us.

And though the world, at last, has swallowed her own
        solemn laughter
And has condemned herself to hell:

Suppose a whole new universe, a great clean Kingdom
Were to rise up like an Atlantis in the East,
Surprise this earth, this cinder, with new holiness!

Here in my hands I hold that secret Easter.
Tomorrow, this will be my Mass's answer,
Because of my companions whom the wilderness has
    eaten,
Crying like Jonas in the belly of our whale.

ELEGY FOR THE MONASTERY BARN

As though an aged person were to wear
Too gay a dress
And walk about the neighborhood
Announcing the hour of her death,

So now, one summer day's end,
At suppertime, when wheels are still,
The long barn suddenly puts on the traitor, beauty,
And hails us with a dangerous cry,
For: "Look!" she calls to the country,
"Look how fast I dress myself in fire!"

Had we half guessed how long her spacious shadows
Harbored a woman's vanity
We would be less surprised to see her now
So loved, and so attended, and so feared.

87

She, in whose airless heart
We burst our veins to fill her full of hay,
Now stands apart.
She will not have us near her. Terribly,
Sweet Christ, how terribly her beauty burns us now!

And yet she has another legacy,
More delicate, to leave us, and more rare.

Who knew her solitude?
Who heard the peace downstairs
While flames ran whispering among the rafters?
Who felt the silence, there,
The long, hushed gallery
Clean and resigned and waiting for the fire?

Look! They have all come back to speak their sum-
        mary:
Fifty invisible cattle, the past years
Assume their solemn places one by one.
This is the little minute of their destiny.
Here is their meaning found. Here is their end.

Laved in the flame as in a Sacrament
The brilliant walls are holy
In their first-last hour of joy.

Fly from within the barn! Fly from the silence
Of this creature sanctified by fire!
Let no man stay inside to look upon the Lord!
Let no man wait within and see the Holy
One sitting in the presence of disaster
Thinking upon this barn His gentle doom!

THE GUNS OF FORT KNOX

Guns at the camp (I hear them suddenly)
Guns make the little houses jump. I feel
Explosions in my feet, through boards.
Wars work under the floor. Wars
Dance in the foundations. Trees
Must also feel the guns they do not want
Even in their core.
As each charge bumps the shocked earth
They shudder from the root.

Shock the hills, you guns! They are
Not too firm even without dynamite.
These Chinese clayfoot hills
Founded in their own shale
Shift their feet in friable stone.

       Such ruins cannot
Keep the armies of the dead
From starting up again.
They'll hear these guns tonight
Tomorrow or some other time.
They'll wake. They'll rise
Through the stunned rocks, form
Regiments and do death's work once more.

Guns, I say, this is not
The right resurrection. All day long
You punch the doors of death to wake
A slain generation. Let them lie

Still. Let them sleep on,
O guns. Shake no more
(But leave the locks secure)
Hell's door.

SPRING STORM

When in their ignorance and haste the skies must fall
Upon our white-eyed home, and blindly turn
Feeling the four long limits of the wall,

How unsubstantial is our present state
In the clean blowing of those elements
Whose study is our problem and our fate?

The intellects go mumbling in the snow,
And find the blurred, incredible sun (and moon)
Jammed in the white door, and the troubled straits
The dugout where the fallen sky lies down.
A mess of secret trumpets, with their weight
Of portents, veil the bluntness where we run.

How true a passion has this hour begun!
The sky melts on my patient animal
(My pointless self, the hunter of my home),
My breath burns in the open like a ton
In the blue waking of those elements
Whose study is our quibble and our doom.

O watch the woolen hundreds on the run!

LANDSCAPE

I

A Personage is seen
Leaning upon a cushion
Printed with cornflowers.

A Child appears
Holding up a pencil.

"This is a picture
(Says the Child to the Personage)
Of the vortex."

"Draw it your own way,"
Says the Personage.

(Music is heard
Pure in the island windows,
Sea-music on the Child's
Interminable shore, his coral home.)

Behind a blue mountain
Covered with chickenfoot trees,
The molten sun appears,
A heavy, painted flower.

A Personage is seen
Leaning upon the mountain
With the sun in one hand
And a pencil in the other.

"This is a picture
(Says the Personage to the Child)
Of the beginning of the world."

"Or of its end!" cries the Child
Hiding himself in the cushions.

2

A Woman appears
Leaning upon the Child's shoulder.
He looks up again.

"This is my Mother
(Says the Child to the Personage)
Older than the moon."

(Grecian horses are heard
Returning from the foam
Of the pure island's windows,
And the Child's horizons.)

"My Mother is a world
(Says the Child to the Personage)
Printed with gillyflowers."

"Paint her your own way"
(Says the Personage to the Child).
And, lifting up his pencil,
He crosses out the sun.

BIRDCAGE WALK

1

One royal afternoon
When I was young and easily surprised
By uncles coming from the park
At the command of nurses and of guards,

I wondered, over trees and ponds,
At the sorry, rude walls
And the white windows of the apartments.
"These," said my uncle, "are the tallest houses."

2

Yes, in the spring of my joy
When I was visibly affected by a gaitered bishop,
Large and unsteady in the flagged yard,
Guards, dogs and blackbirds fled on every hand.

"He is an old one," said uncle,
"The gaiters are real."

3

Rippled, fistfed windows of your
Dun high houses! Then
Come cages made of pretty willows
Where they put the palace girls!
Green ducks wade slowly from the marble water.
One swan reproves a saucy daughter.

I consider my own true pond,
Look for the beginning and the end.
I lead the bishop down lanes and islands.

4

Yes, in the windows of my first existence
Before my yawns became seasons,
When nurses and uncles were sure,
Chinese fowl fought the frosty water
Startled by this old pontifex.

"No bridge" (He smiled
Between the budding branches),
"No crossing to the cage
Of the paradise bird!"

Astounded by the sermons in the leaves
I cried, "No! No! The stars have higher houses!"

Kicking the robins and ganders
From the floor of his insular world
The magic bishop leaned his blessing on the children.

That was the bold day when
Moved by the unexpected summons
I opened all the palace aviaries
As by a king's representative
I was appointed fowler.

WISDOM

I studied it and it taught me nothing.
I learned it and soon forgot everything else:
Having forgotten, I was burdened with knowledge—
The insupportable knowledge of nothing.

How sweet my life would be, if I were wise!
Wisdom is well known
When it is no longer seen or thought of.
Only then is understanding bearable.

TO A SEVERE NUN

I know, Sister, that solitude
Will never dismay you. You have chosen
A path too steep for others to follow.
I take it you prefer to go without them.

You will not complain that others are fickle
When they abandon you, renouncing the contest.
After all, they have not understood
That love is a contest, and that the love you demand
Is a match, in which you overcome your friends
After a long agony.

Thus you have no visible companions. Yet, drive on,
Drive on: do not consider your despair! Imagine
    rather
That there are many saints around you in the same
    desperation,
Violent, without contact, without responsibility,
Except of course to their own just souls
And to the God Who cannot blame them.

You know where you are going. You alone
In the whole convent know what bitter comfort
Eludes the malcontents who travel this unusual desert,
Seeking the impossible, and not the Absolute—
Sustained always by the same hate.

Do not be disconcerted, Sister, if in spite of your effort
The impertinent truth shows up weakness at least in
    others
And distracts you with their suffering.
Do not be humbled if, for an instant,
Christ seems glad to suffer in another.

Forget this scandal. Do not look at them
Or you may lose your nerve, and come to admit
That violence is your evasion and that you,
You most of all, are weak.

"WHEN IN THE SOUL OF THE SERENE DISCIPLE . . ."

When in the soul of the serene disciple
With no more Fathers to imitate
Poverty is a success,
It is a small thing to say the roof is gone:
He has not even a house.

Stars, as well as friends,
Are angry with the noble ruin.
Saints depart in several directions.

Be still:
There is no longer any need of comment.
It was a lucky wind
That blew away his halo with his cares,
A lucky sea that drowned his reputation.

Here you will find
Neither a proverb nor a memorandum.
There are no ways,
No methods to admire
Where poverty is no achievement.
His God lives in his emptiness like an affliction.

What choice remains?
Well, to be ordinary is not a choice:
It is the usual freedom
Of men without visions.

A PRACTICAL PROGRAM FOR MONKS

1

Each one shall sit at table with his own cup and
  spoon, and with his own repentance. Each one's
  own business shall be his most important affair,
  and provide his own remedies.
They have neglected bowl and plate.
Have you a wooden fork?
Yes, each monk has a wooden fork as well as a potato.

2

Each one shall wipe away tears with his own saint,
  when three bells hold in store a hot afternoon.
  Each one is supposed to mind his own heart, with
  its conscience, night and morning.
Another turn on the wheel: ho hum! And observe the
  Abbot!
Time to go to bed in a straw blanket.

3

Plenty of bread for everyone between prayers and the
  psalter: will you recite another?
Merci, and *Miserere.*
Always mind both the clock and the Abbot until
  eternity.
Miserere.

4

Details of the Rule are all liquid and solid. What
  canon was the first to announce regimentation
  before us? Mind the step on the way down!

Yes, I dare say you are right, Father. I believe you; I
    believe you.
I believe it is easier when they have ice water and even
    a lemon.
Each one can sit at table with his own lemon, and
    mind his conscience.

5

Can we agree that the part about the lemon is regu-
    lar?
In any case, it is better to have sheep than peacocks,
    and cows rather than a chained leopard says
    Modest, in one of his proverbs.
The monastery, being owner of a communal row-
    boat, is the antechamber of heaven.
Surely that ought to be enough.

6

Each one can have some rain after Vespers on a hot
    afternoon, but *ne quid nimis,* or the purpose of
    the Order will be forgotten.
We shall send you hyacinths and a sweet millennium.
Everything the monastery provides is very pleasant to
    see and to sell for nothing.
What is baked smells fine. There is a sign of God on
    every leaf that nobody sees in the garden. The
    fruit trees are there on purpose, even when no
    one is looking. Just put the apples in the basket.
In Kentucky there is also room for a little cheese.
Each one shall fold his own napkin, and neglect the
    others.

7

Rain is always very silent in the night, under such
    gentle cathedrals.
Yes, I have taken care of the lamp. *Miserere*.
Have you a patron saint, and an angel?
Thank you. Even though the nights are never danger-
    ous, I have one of everything.

SONG: IN THE SHOWS OF THE
ROUND OX

i

In the shows of the round Ox
(O pagan night)
They fought their lucky stars.

Light of a wicked sun
And flying cars.

In the shows of the brass barn
(O fatal sun)
They lost a morning's fortune.

ii
"There is no game like money"
(Cries the man with the hand)
"So sell your brother".

Light of a gambling clock
And trained symbols.
When they win, they drown.

"There is no game like homeward"
Cry the whirlwind trumpeters.

iii
To the shallow water
They are standing on
These waterwalkers owe
No genuine fortune.

Strong ones have their own
Problems and pardons
For the iron ox.

iv
Tell me the name of the brass horn
That makes all the money.
Tell me the day of the wargames
Where gold is won.
The winning day is the day
On my green paper.
The first-last dollar's number
Is my own name.

v
The brass fighting cocks
And bloodred winners
Ask no pardon
And present no problem.

(But there is no game like pardon).

vi
The fight is over. Eyes of the furious Ox
Are brass suns. There is no game like standing on the
    water:

But there is no winner.

Strong ones have their own
Mercies and questions
For brazen fortune.

AN ELEGY FOR FIVE OLD LADIES

*(Newton, Mass., April 20: Five women ranging in age from 80
to 96 drowned this afternoon when a driverless car rolled across a
rest home lawn and sank in Crystal Lake . . .* THE NEW YORK
TIMES)

Let us forget that it is spring and celebrate the rider-
    less will of five victims.
Old companions are sitting silent in the home. Five of
    their number have suddenly gone too far, as if
    waifs,

As if orphans were to swim without license. Their ride was not lucky. It took them very far out of bounds.

Mrs. Watson said she saw them all go at three forty five. Their bell had rung too loud and too late.

It was a season when water is too cold for anyone, and is especially icy for an old person.

The brazen sedan was not to be trusted. The wheels went too well for one short and straight journey. It was the last: the doors did not open.

Dimly and too late they saw themselves on a very wicked lawn. May God have mercy on their recreation!

Let us accordingly pay homage to five now legendary persons, the very chaste daughters of one unlucky ride.

Let the perversity of a machine become our common study, while I name loudly five loyal spouses of death!

POETRY AND CONTEMPLATION:
A Reappraisal

POETRY AND CONTEMPLATION:
A REAPPRAISAL

Author's note: Ten years ago I wrote an article called "Poetry and the Contemplative Life" which was published first in The Commonweal and then appeared in a volume of verse, *Figures for an Apocalypse*.

In its original form, this article stated a "problem" and tried to apply a rather crude "solution" which, at the time, was rather widely discussed by people interested in religious verse and, at least by implication, in religious experience. Many of them were inclined to accept the "solution" that was proposed. Others wisely rejected it because of its somewhat puritanical implications.

As time passed I have found that the confident pronouncements made in my early writing lay more and more heavily on my conscience as a writer and as a priest, and while it is evidently impossible to correct and amend all my wrong-headed propositions, at least I would like to revise the essay of 1948. The revision is unfortunately not fully satisfactory precisely because it is no more than a revision. But I do not want to write a whole new article, approaching the subject from an entirely different angle. I believe it is necessary to revise the earlier article and to restate the case in the same context, arriving at a different conclusion.

One of the unavoidable defects of this kind of revision is that it retains an altogether misleading insistence on the terms "contemplation" and "contemplative life" as something apart from the rest of man's existence. This involves a rather naive presupposition that "contemplation" is a kind of objectivized entity which gets "interfered with" by such things as esthetic reflection. There is a certain amount of truth behind this supposed conflict, but to state it thus crudely is to invite all sorts of misunderstanding. In actual fact, neither religious nor artistic contemplation should be regarded as "things" which happen or "objects" which one can "have." They belong to the much more mysterious realm of what one "is"— or rather "who" one is. Esthetic intuition is not merely the act of a faculty, it is also a heightening and intensification of our personal identity and being by the perception of our connatural affinity with "Being" in the beauty contemplated.

But also, and at the same time, the implied conflict between "contemplation" as rest and poetic creation as activity is even more misleading. It is all wrong to imagine that in order to "contemplate" divine things or what you will, it is necessary to abstain from every kind of action and enter into a kind of spiritual stillness where one waits for "something to happen." In actual fact, true contemplation is inseparable from life and from the dynamism of life—which includes work, creation, production, fruitfulness and above all *love*. Contemplation is not to be thought of as a separate department of life, cut off from all man's other interests and superseding them. It is the very fullness of a fully integrated life. It is the crown of life and of all life's activities.

Therefore the earlier problem was, largely, an illusion, created by this division of life into formally separate compartments, of "action" and "contemplation." But because this crude division was stated so forcefully and so frequently in my earlier writings, I feel that it is most necessary now to try to do something to heal this wound and draw together the two sides of this unfortunate fissure.

In this present article, the wound is still evident, and it is meant to be so. I am attempting to patch it up, and probably do not fully succeed. If this is true, I do not care so much, as long as it is clear that I am stitching and drawing the wound together, pouring in the disinfectant, and putting on a bandage.

I

In an age of science and technology, in which man finds himself bewildered and disoriented by the fabulous versatility of the machines he has created, we live precipitated outside ourselves at every moment, interiorly empty, spiritually lost, seeking at all costs to forget our own emptiness, and ready to alienate ourselves completely in the name of any "cause" that comes along. At such a time as this, it seems absurd to talk of contemplation: and indeed a great deal of the talk that has been bandied about timidly enough on this subject, is ludicrous and inadequate. Contemplation itself takes on the appearance of a safe and rather bourgeois "cause"—the refuge of a few well-meaning Christians who are willing to acquaint themselves with St. Thomas and St. John of the Cross, and to disport themselves thereafter in such Edens of passivity and fervor as cannot be disapproved by the so-called "Masters of the Spiritual Life". For others, safer still, contemplation means nothing more than a life of leisure and of study: in many cases more a fond hope than an accomplished fact.

The relative timidity of these adventures, and the hare-brained chase after more exotic forms of spirituality, should not make us too prone to laugh at every symptom of man's acute need for an interior life. For one of the most important and most hopeful signs of the times is in the turbulent, anarchic, but fully determined efforts of a small minority of men to recover some kind of contact with their own inner depths, to recapture the freshness and truth of their own subjectivity, and to go on from there not only to God, but to the spirit of other men. In the face of our own almost hopeless alienation, we are trying to get back to ourselves before it is too late. One of the most outstanding examples of this struggle is seen in the almost symbolic career of Boris Pasternak whose more recent poetry and prose can most certainly qualify in a broad and basic sense as *contemplative*.

The contemplative is not just a man who sits under a tree with his legs crossed, or one who edifies himself with the answer to ultimate and spiritual problems. He is one who seeks to know the meaning of life not only with his head but with his whole being, by living it in depth and in purity and thus uniting himself to the very Source of Life—a Source which is infinitely actual and therefore too real to be contained satisfactorily inside any word or concept or name assigned by man: for the words of man tend to limit the realities which they express, in order to express them. And anything that can be limited cannot be the infinite actuality known to the contemplative without words and without the mediation of precise analytical thought. We can say, then, that contemplation is the intuitive perception of life in its Source: that Source Who revealed Himself as the unnameable "I Am" and then again made Himself known to us as Man in Christ. Contemplation is experience of God in Man, God in the world, God in Christ: it is an obscure intuition of God Himself, and this intuition is a gift of God Who reveals Himself in His very hiddenness as One unknown.

Contemplation is related to art, to worship, to charity: all these reach out by intuition and self-dedication into the realms that transcend the material conduct of everyday life. Or rather, in the midst of ordinary life itself they seek and find a new and transcendent meaning. And by this meaning they transfigure the whole of life. Art, worship, and love penetrate into the spring of living waters that flows from the depths where man's spirit is united to God, and draw from those depths power to create a new world and a new life. Contemplation goes deeper than all three, and unites them, and plunges man's whole soul into the supernal waters, in the baptism of wordless understanding and ecstatic prayer.

There can be various levels of contemplation. There is contemplation in a broad and improper sense—the religious intuition of the artist, the lover or the worshipper. In these intuitions, art, love or worship remain in the foreground: they modify the experience of ultimate reality, and present that reality to us as the "object" of aesthetic vision, or adoration, or love. In an even less proper sense, "contemplation" loses sight of ultimates and becomes preoccupied with a beautiful thing, or a meaningful liturgy, or a loved person.

But in its proper meaning, contemplation transcends all "objects", all "things" and goes beyond all "ideas" of beauty or goodness or truth, passes beyond all speculation, all creative fervor, all charitable action, and "rests" in the inexpressible. It lets go of everything and finds All in Nothing—the *todo y nada* of St. John of the Cross.

On a dark night, kindled in love with yearnings—
     oh happy chance—
I went forth without being observed, my house being
     now at rest.

In darkness and secure, by the secret ladder, disguised,
     —O happy chance—
In darkness and concealment, my house being now at
rest.

In the happy night, in secret when none saw me
Nor I beheld aught, without light or guide save that
   which burned in my heart

This light guided me more surely than the light of
   noonday
To the place where He (well I knew who!) was
   awaiting me
A place where none appeared.

Now when we speak of a possible conflict between
poetry and contemplation, it is clearly only contemplation in the last, most perfect sense, that is intended. For when we speak of contemplation in the
more broad and improper sense, we find it uniting itself with art, with worship and with love. It is not
only compatible with poetic creation, but is stimulated
by it, and in its turn inspires poetry. And in the realm
of worship, contemplation in this broad sense is stimulated by meditation, by prayer, by liturgy, and arises
out of these religious activities. Above all, in the sacramental life of the Church, we find contemplation in
this broad sense should normally be the fruit of
fervent reception of the sacraments, at least sometimes. That is to say that the reception of the sacraments should produce, once in a while, not only interior and unfelt grace but also a certain dim awareness of the presence and the action of God in the
soul, though this awareness may be very fleeting,
tenuous and almost impossible to assess. Nor should
people trouble their heads about whether or not they

feel it, because some are not supposed to feel it: feelings are not important, and what they will experience without realizing it too clearly, is the fervor of love and the desire to dedicate themselves more perfectly to God. Such things we can call in a broad and improper sense "contemplative" experiences.

This is *active* contemplation, in which grace indeed is the principle of all the supernatural value and ordination of our acts, but in which much of the initiative belongs to our own powers, prompted and sustained by grace. This form of the contemplative life prepares us for contemplation properly so called: the life of *infused* or *passive* or *mystical* contemplation.

Contemplation is the fullness of the Christian vocation—the full flowering of baptismal grace and of the Christ-life in our souls.

Christian contemplation is not something esoteric and dangerous. It is simply the experience of God that is given to a soul purified by humility and faith. It is the "knowledge" of God in the darkness of infused love. "This is eternal life, that they should know Thee, the One True God, and Jesus Christ Whom Thou hast sent" (John 17:3) or "But we all, beholding the glory of the Lord with open face, are transformed into the same image from glory to glory, as by the Spirit of the Lord." (2 Corinthians 3:18). St. Paul, in his Epistle to the Hebrews, rebuked those who clung to the "first elements of the words of God" when they should have been "Masters," and he urged them to relinquish the "milk" of beginners and to desire the "strong meat" of the perfect, which is the contemplation of Christ in the great Mystery in which He renews on earth the redemptive sacrifice of the Cross. "For every one that is a partaker of milk is unskillful in the word of justice: for he is a little child. But strong meat is for the perfect: for them who by custom have their senses exercised to the discerning of good and evil" (Hebrews 5:13-14). *Omnis qui ad Dominum convertitur contemplativam vitam desiderat,* said St. Gregory the Great, and he was using contemplation in our sense: to live on the desire of God alone; to have one's mind divested of all earthly things and united, insofar as human weakness permits, with Christ. And he adds that the contemplative life begins on earth in order to continue, more perfectly, in heaven. St. Thomas echoed him with his famous phrase: *quaedam inchoatio beatitudinis* (Contemplation is a beginning of eternal blessedness). St. Bonaventure goes further than any of the other Doctors of the Church in his insistence that all Christians should desire union with God in loving contemplation. And in his second conference on the Hexaemeron, applying Christ's words in Matthew 12:42, he says that the Queen of the South who left her own land and traveled far to hear the wisdom of Solomon will rise up in judgment against our generation which refuses the treasure of divine wisdom, preferring the far lesser riches of worldly wisdom and philosophy.

Infused contemplation is a quasi-experimental knowledge of God's goodness "tasted" and "possessed" by a vital contact in the depths of the soul. By infused love, we are given an immediate grasp of God's own substance, and rest in the obscure and profound sense of His presence and transcendent actions within our inmost selves, yielding ourselves altogether to the work of His transforming Spirit.

By the light of infused wisdom we enter deeply into the Mystery of Christ Who is Himself the light of men. We participate, as it were, in the glory that is radiated mystically by His risen and transfigured Humanity. Our eyes are opened to understand the Scriptures and the mystery of God's intervention in man's history. We become aware of the way in which the infinite mercy and wisdom of God are revealed to men and angels in the Mystery of the Church, which is the Body of Christ. The contemplative life is the lot of those who have entered most fully into the life and spirit of the Church, so that the contemplatives are at the very heart of the Mystery which they have begun really to understand and to "see" with the eyes of their soul. To desire the contemplative life and its gifts is therefore to desire to become in the highest sense a fruitful and strong member of Christ. But it means also, by that very fact, to desire and accept a share in His sufferings and death, that we may rise with Him in the participation of His glory.

Now whether we speak of contemplation as active or passive, one thing is evident: it brings us into the closest contact with the one subject that is truly worthy of a Christian poet: the great Mystery of God, revealing His mercy to us in Christ. The Christian poet should be one who has been granted a deep understanding of the ways of God and of the Mystery of Christ. Deeply rooted in the spiritual consciousness of the whole Church, steeped in the Liturgy and the Scriptures, fully possessed by the "mind of the Church," he becomes as it were a voice of the Church and of the Holy Spirit, and sings again the *magnalia Dei,* praising God and pointing out the wonder of His ways. The Christian poet is therefore the successor to David and the Prophets, he contemplates what was announced by the poets of the Old Testament: he should be, as they were, a mystic, full of divine fire. He should be one who, like the prophet Isaias, has seen the living God and has lamented the fact that he was a man of impure lips, until God Himself sent Seraph, with a live coal from the altar of the heavenly temple, to burn his lips with prophetic inspiration.

In the true Christian poet—in Dante, St. John of the Cross, St. Francis, Jacopone da Todi, Hopkins, Paul Claudel—we find it hard to distinguish between the inspiration of the prophet and mystic, and the purely poetic enthusiasm of great artistic genius.

Consider also what a tremendous mine of literary inspiration is in the Liturgical life. The Liturgy itself contains the greatest literature, not only from Scripture, but from the genius of the Patristic and Middle Ages. The Liturgy stands at the crossroads of the natural and supernatural lives, and exploits all the possibilities of both in order to bring out every possible meaning and implication that is in them with respect to our salvation and the praise of God. It surrounds those founts of all supernatural vitality, the Sacraments, with a music that is perfect in its integrity and dignity, and with ceremonies that are most meaningful by reason of their tremendous, dramatic simplicity, not to mention all the resources of pictorial and plastic art still unknown in this land which has never yet possessed a Chartres or an Assisi.

The Liturgy is, then, not only a school of literary taste and a mine of marvelous subjects, but it is infinitely more: it is a sacramental system built around the greatest Sacrament, the Blessed Eucharist, in which Christ Himself is enthroned, in mystery, in the very heart of His wonderful creation.

Christ on the Cross is the fount of all art because He is the Word, the fount of all grace and wisdom. He is the center of everything, of the whole economy of the natural and the supernatural orders. Everything that is made subsists in Him and reflects His beauty. Everything points to this anointed King of Creation Who is the splendor of the eternal light and the mirror of the Godhead without stain. He is the "image of the invisible God, the firstborn of every creature . . . in Him were all things created, by Him and in Him . . . He is before all and by Him all things consist . . . in Whom it hath pleased the Father that all things should dwell . . . for in Him dwelleth all the fulness of the Godhead corporeally," that in all things He may hold the primacy. (Colossians, 1 and 2.)

The Christian's vision of the world ought, by its very nature, to have in it something of poetic inspiration. Our faith ought to be capable of filling our hearts with a wonder and a wisdom which see beyond the surface of things and events, and grasp something of the inner and "sacred" meaning of the cosmos which, in all its movements and all its aspects, sings the praises of its Creator and Redeemer.

No Christian poetry worthy of the name has been written by anyone who was not in some degree a contemplative. I say "in some degree" because obviously not all Christian poets are mystics. But the true poet is always akin to the mystic because of the "prophetic" intuition by which he sees the spiritual reality, the inner meaning of the object he contemplates, which makes that concrete reality not only a thing worthy of admiration in itself, but also and above all makes it a *sign of God*. All good Christian poets are then contemplatives in the sense that they see God everywhere in His creation and in His mysteries, and behold the created world as filled with signs and symbols of God. To the true Christian poet, the whole world and all the incidents of life tend to be sacraments—signs of God, signs of His love working in the world.

However, the mere fact of having this contemplative vision of God in the world around us does not necessarily make a man a great poet. One must be not a "seer" but also and especially a "creator"—a "maker." Poetry is an art, a natural skill, a virtue of

119

the practical intellect, and no matter how great a subject we may have in the experience of contemplation, we will not be able to put it into words if we do not have the proper command of our medium. This is true. But let us assume that a man already has this natural gift. If the inspiration is helpless without a correspondingly effective technique, technique is barren without inspiration.

2

Christ is the inspiration of Christian poetry, and Christ is at the center of the contemplative life. Therefore, it would seem fairly evident that the one thing that will most contribute to the perfection of Catholic literature in general and poetry in particular will be for our writers and poets to live more as "contemplatives" than as citizens of a materialistic world. This means first of all leading the full Christian sacramental and liturgical life insofar as they can in their state. Obviously, the poet does not have to enter a monastery to be a better poet. On the contrary, what we need are "contemplatives" outside the cloister and outside the rigidly fixed patterns of religious life—contemplatives in the world of art, letters, education, and even politics. This means a solid integration of one's work, thought, religion, and family life and recreations in one vital harmonious unity with Christ at its center. The liturgical life is the most obvious example of "active contemplation," but it is hard enough to find a parish where the liturgical life is anything more than a bare skeleton. The eccentricities and obsessions of occasional faddists should not prejudice us against the immense vitality and permanent value of the true liturgical revival. It is quite certain that one of the most valid achievements in the realm of Christian art in our time is to the credit of the Monks of Solesmes, with their revival of Gregorian chant.

A sincere and efficacious desire to enter more deeply into the beauty of the Christian mystery implies a willingness to sacrifice the things which are called "beautiful" by the decadent standards of a materialistic world. Yet the Christian contemplative need not confine himself to religious, still less to professionally "pious" models. He will, of course, read Scripture and above all the contemplative saints: John of the Cross, Teresa of Avila, John Ruysbroek, Bonaventure, Bernard. But no one can be a poet without reading the good poets of his own time—T. S. Eliot, Auden, Spender, Rilke, Pasternak, Dylan Thomas, Garcia Lorca. One might add that a fully integrated vision of our time and of its spirit presupposes some contact with the genius of Baudelaire and Rimbaud, who are Christians turned inside out.

Contemplation has much to offer poetry. And poetry, in its turn, has something to offer contemplation. How is this so? In understanding the relation of poetry to contemplation the first thing that needs to be stressed is the essential dignity of esthetic experience. It is, in itself, a very high gift, though only in the natural order. It is a gift which very many people have never received, and which others, having received, have allowed to spoil or become atrophied within them through neglect and misuse.

To many people, the enjoyment of art is nothing more than a sensible and emotional thrill. They look at a picture, and if it stimulates one or another of their sense-appetites they are pleased. On a hot day they like to look at a picture of mountains or the sea because it makes them feel cool. They like paintings of dogs that you could almost pat. But naturally they soon tire of art, under those circumstances. They turn aside to pat a real dog, or they go down the street to an air-conditioned movie, to give their senses another series of jolts. This is not what one can legitimately call the "enjoyment of Art."

A genuine esthetic experience is something which transcends not only the sensible order (in which, however, it has its beginning) but also that of reason itself. It is a supra-rational intuition of the latent perfection of things. Its immediacy outruns the speed of reasoning and leaves all analysis far behind. In the natural order, as Jacques Maritain has often insisted, it is an analogue of the mystical experience which it resembles and imitates from afar. Its mode of apprehension is that of "connaturality"—it reaches out to grasp the inner reality, the vital substance of its object, by a kind of affective identification of itself with it. It rests in the perfection of things by a kind of union which sometimes resembles the quiescence of the soul in its immediate affective contact with God in the obscurity of mystical prayer. A true artist can contemplate a picture for hours, and it is a real contemplation, too. So close is the resemblance between these two experiences that a poet like Blake could almost confuse the two and make them merge into one another as if they belonged to the same order of things.

This resemblance between the experiences of the artist and of the mystic has been extensively discussed in the long and important article on "Art and Spirituality," by Fr. M. Leonard, S. J., in the *Dictionnaire de Spiritualité*.

This theologian pushes the dignity of the esthetic institution practically to its limit. He gives it everything that it is ontologically able to stand. He insists that the highest experience of the artist penetrates not only beyond the sensible surface of things into their inmost reality, but even beyond that to God Himself. More than that, the analogy with mystical experience is deeper and closer still because, he says, the intuition of the artist sets in motion the very same psychological processes which accompany infused contemplation. This would seem to be too much: but no, it is not. It fits in with the psychology of St. Augustine and St. Bonaventure and the latter's notion of contemplation *per speculum,* passing through the mirror of created things to God, even if that mirror may happen to be our own soul. It also fits in with the ideas of the Greek Fathers about *theoria physica* or "natural contemplation" which arrives at God through the inner spiritual reality (the *logos*) of the created thing.

The Augustinian psychology, which forms the traditional substratum of Christian mystical theology in the Western Church, distinguishes between an *inferior* and *superior* soul. Of course, this is only a manner of speaking. There is only one soul, a simple spiritual substance, undivided and indivisible. And yet the soul insofar as it acts through its faculties, making decisions and practical judgments concerning temporal external things, is called "inferior." The "superior" soul is the same soul, but now considered as the principle or *actus primus* of these other diverse and multiple acts of the faculties which as it were flow from this inner principle. Only the superior soul is strictly the image of God within us. And if we are to contemplate God at all, this internal image must be re-formed by grace, and then we must enter into this inner sanctuary which is the substance of the soul itself. This passage from the exterior to the interior has nothing to do with concentration or introspection. It is a transit from objectivization to knowledge by intuition and connaturality. The majority of people never enter into this inward self, which is an abode of silence and peace and where the diversified activities of the intellect and will are collected, so to speak, into one intense and smooth and spiritualized activity which far exceeds in its fruitfulness the plodding efforts of reason working on external reality with its analyses and syllogisms.

It is here that mystical contemplation begins. It is into this substance or "center" of the soul, when it has transcended its dependence on sensations and images and concepts, that the obscure light of infused contemplation will be poured by God, giving us experimental contact with Himself without the medium of sense species. And in this contact, we are no longer facing God as an "object" of experience or as a concept which we apprehend. We are united to Him in the mystery of love and its transcendent subjectivity, and see Him in ourselves by losing ourselves in Him.

Yet even in the natural order, without attaining to God in us, and without perceiving this "inner spiritual light," the esthetic experience introduces us into the interior sanctuary of the soul and to its inexpressible simplicity. For the esthetic intuition is also beyond objectivity—it "sees" by identifying itself spiritually with what it contemplates.

Obviously, then, when the natural contemplation of the artist or the metaphysician has already given a man a taste of the peaceful intoxication which is experienced in the supra-rational intuitions of this interior self, the way is already well prepared for infused contemplation. If God should grant that grace, the person so favored will be much better prepared to recognize it, and to cooperate with God's action within him. This, as a matter of fact, is a tremendous advantage. The artist, the poet, the metaphysician is, then, in some sense already naturally prepared and disposed to remove some of the principal obstacles to the light of infused contemplation. He will be less tempted than the ordinary man to reach out for vulgar satisfactions and imaginable thrills. He will be more "spiritual," if not more "religious." He will be more ready to keep himself detached from the level of crude feeling and emotionalism which so easily corrupt the integrity both of the artist and of the man of prayer. The mere fact of the artist's or poet's good taste, which should belong to him by virtue of his art, will help him to avoid some of the evils that tend to corrupt religious experience before it has a chance to take root and grow in the soul.

3

Mystical contemplation is absolutely beyond the reach of man's natural activity. There is nothing he can do to obtain it by himself. It is a pure gift of God. God gives it to whom He wills, and in the way and degree in which He wills. By cooperating with the work of ordinary grace we can—and, if we really mean to love God, we must—seek Him and even find Him obscurely by a love that gropes humbly for truth in the darkness of this life. But no amount of generosity on our part, no amount of effort, no amount of sacrifice will make us into mystics. That is a work that must be done by God acting as the "principal agent" (the term is that of St. John of the Cross). If He is the principal agent, there is another agent: ourselves. But our part is simply to consent, to listen and to follow without knowing where we are going. All the rest that we can do amounts to the more or less negative task of avoiding obstacles and keeping our own prejudiced judgments and self-will out of His way. St. Bonaventure tells us in many places that prayer and ardent desire can persuade God to give us this gift, and that *industria* on our part can open the way for His action. The term *industria* stands for active purification, and St. Bonaventure means, by that, precisely the same thing that St. John of the Cross talks about all through the "Ascent of Mount Carmel," namely the active emptying of the soul, clearing it of all images, all likenesses of and attachments to created things so that it may be clean and pure to receive the obscure light of God's own presence. The soul must be stripped of all its selfish desires for natural satisfactions, no matter how high, how noble or how excellent in themselves. As long as it rests in things for their own sake, seen and possessed as "objects" to gratify our own self-love, it cannot possess God and be possessed by Him, for the love of the soul for objectivized beings is darkness in the sight of God.

It is the common doctrine of Christian mystical theologians that a great obstacle to "unitive" or "connatural" or "affective" knowledge of God by infused contemplation (the terms are those of St. Thomas and his followers) is attachment to objectivized human reasoning and analysis and discourse that proceeds by abstraction from sense images, and by syllogizing, to conclusions. In other words, a man cannot at the same time fly in an airplane and walk along the ground. He must do one or the other. And if he insists on walking along the ground—all right, it is no sin. But it will take him much longer and cost him much more effort to get to his destination, and he will have a much more limited view of things along his way. What the Holy Spirit demands of the mystic is peaceful consent, and a blind trust in Him: for all this time, since the soul does not act of itself, it remains blind and in darkness, having no idea where it is going or what is being done, and tasting satisfaction that is, at first, extremely tenuous and ineffable and obscure. The reason is, of course, that the soul is not yet sufficiently spiritualized to be able to grasp and appreciate what is going on within it. It remains with nothing but the vaguest and most general sense that God is really and truly present and working there—a sense which is fraught with a greater certitude than anything it has ever experienced before. And yet if one stops to analyze the experience, or if one makes a move to increase its intensity by a natural act, the whole thing will evade his grasp and he will lose it altogether.

Now it is precisely here that the esthetic instinct changes its colors and, from being a precious gift, becomes a real danger. If the intuition of the poet naturally leads him into the inner sanctuary of his soul, it is for a special purpose in the natural order: when the poet enters into himself, it is in order to reflect upon his inspiration and to clothe it with a special and splendid form and then return to *display it to those outside*. And here the radical difference between the artist and the mystic begins to be seen. The artist enters into himself in order to *work*. For him, the "superior" soul is a forge where inspiration kindles a fire of white heat, a crucible for the transformation of natural images into new, created forms. But the mystic enters into himself, not in order to work but to pass through the center of his own soul and lose himself in the mystery and secrecy and infinite, transcendent reality of God living and working within him.

Consequently, if the mystic happens to be, at the same time, an artist, when prayer calls him within himself to the secrecy of God's presence, his art will be tempted to start working and producing and studying the "creative" possibilities of this experience. And therefore immediately the whole thing runs the risk of being frustrated and destroyed. The artist will run the risk of losing a gift of tremendous supernatural worth, in order to perform a work of far less value. He will let go of the deep, spiritual grace which has been granted him, in order to return to the reflection of that grace within his own soul. He will withdraw from the mystery of identification with Reality beyond forms and objectivized concepts, and will return to the realm of subject and object. He will objectivize his own experience and seek to exploit and employ it for its own sake. He will leave God and return to himself, and in so doing, though he follows his natural instinct to "create" he will, in fact, be less creative. For the creative work done directly in the soul and on the soul by God Himself, the infinite *Creator Spiritus,* is beyond all comparison with the work which the soul of man itself accomplishes in imitation of the divine Creator.

Unable fully to lose himself in God, doomed by the restlessness of talent to seek himself in the highest natural gift that God has given him, the artist falls from contemplation and returns to himself as artist. Instead of passing through his own soul into the abyss of the infinite actuality of God Himself, he will remain there a moment, only to emerge again into the exterior world of multiple created things whose variety once more dissipates his energies until they are lost in perplexity and dissatisfaction.

There is, therefore, a likelihood that one who has the natural gift of artistic intuition and creation may be unable to pass on to the superior and most spiritual kind of contemplation, in which the soul rests in God without images, without concepts, without any intermediary. The artist may be like the hare in the fable, who far outstrips the tortoise without talent in the beginnings of the contemplative life, but who, in the end, is left behind. In a word, natural gifts and talents may be of great value in the beginning, but contemplation can never depend on them. They may, indeed, prove to be obstacles, unless by some special grace we are completely detached from them. And so the artist may well receive the first taste of infused prayer, for, as St. John of the Cross says, that is granted to relatively many souls, and often quite soon in their spiritual life, especially where conditions are favorable: but, because of this tragic promethean tendency to exploit every experience as material for "creation" the artist may remain there all his life on the threshold, never entering into the banquet, but always running back into the street to tell the passers-by of the wonderful music he has heard coming from inside the palace of the King!

4

What, then, is the conclusion? That poetry can, indeed, help to bring us rapidly through that early part of the journey to contemplation that is called active: but when we are entering the realm of true contemplation, where eternal happiness is tasted in anticipation, poetic intuition may ruin our rest in God "beyond all images."

In such an event, one might at first be tempted to say that there is only one course for the poet to take, if he wants to be a mystic or a saint: he must consent to the *ruthless and complete sacrifice of his art*. Such a conclusion would seem to be dictated by logic. If there is an infinite distance between the gifts of nature and those of grace, between the natural and the supernatural order, man and God, then should not one always reject the natural for the supernatural, the temporal for the eternal, the human for the divine? It seems to be so simple as to defy contradiction. And yet, when one has experience in the strange vicissitudes of the inner life, and when one has seen something of the ways of God, one remembers that there is a vast difference between the logic of men and the logic of God. There is indeed no human logic in the ways of interior prayer, only Divine paradox. Our God is not a Platonist. Our Christian spirituality is not the intellectualism of Plotinus or the asceticism of the stoics. We must therefore be very careful of over-simplifications. The Christian is sanctified not merely by always making the choice of "the most perfect thing." Indeed, experience teaches us that the most perfect choice is not always that which is most perfect in itself. The most perfect choice is *the choice of what God has willed for us,* even though it may be, in itself, less perfect, and indeed less "spiritual."

It is quite true that esthetic experience is only a temporal thing, and like all other temporal things it passes away. It is true that mystical prayer enriches man a hundredfold in time and in eternity. It purifies the soul and loads it with supernatural merits, enlarging man's powers and capacities to absorb the infinite rivers of divine light which will one day be his beatitude. The sacrifice of art would seem to be a small enough price to lay down for this "pearl of great price."

But let us consider for a moment whether the Christian contemplative poet is necessarily confronted with an absolute clean-cut "either/or" choice between "art" and "mystical prayer."

It can of course happen that a contemplative and artist finds himself in a situation in which he is morally certain that God demands of him the sacrifice of his art, in order that he may enter more deeply into the contemplative life. In such a case, the sacrifice must be made, not because this is a general law binding all artist-contemplatives, but because it is the will of God in this particular, concrete case.

But it may equally well happen that an artist who imagines himself to be called to the higher reaches of mystical prayer is not called to them at all. It becomes evident, to him, that the simplest and most obvious thing for him is to be an artist, and that he should sacrifice his aspirations for a deep mystical life and be content with the lesser gifts with which he has been endowed by God. For such a one, to insist on spending long hours in prayer frustrating his creative instinct would, in fact, lead to illusion. His efforts to be a contemplative would be fruitless. Indeed, he would find that by being an artist—and at the same time living fully all the implications of art for a Christian and for a contemplative in the broad sense of the word —he would enjoy a far deeper and more vital interior life, with a much richer appreciation of the mysteries of God, than if he just tried to bury his artistic talent and be a professional "saint." If he is called to be an artist, then his art will lead him to sanctity, if he uses it as a Christian should.

To take yet another case: it might conceivably be the will of God—as it certainly was in the case of the Old Testament Prophets and in that of St. John of the Cross—that a man should remain *at the same time a mystic and a poet* and ascend to the greatest heights of poetic creation and of mystical prayer without any evident contradiction between them. Here again, the problem is solved not by the application of some abstract, *a priori* principle, but purely by a practically practical appeal to the will of God in this particular case. We are dealing with gifts of God, which God can give as He pleases, when He pleases, to whom He pleases. It is futile for us to lay down laws which say when or how God's gifts must be given, to whom they can be given, to whom they must be refused. It remains true that at a certain point in the interior life, the instinct to create and communicate enters into conflict with the call to mystical union with God. But God Himself can resolve the conflict. And He does. Nor does He need any advice from us in order to do so.

The Christian life is the life of Christ in the soul. Christian wisdom is the wisdom of God's only-begotten Son, Who is begotten Wisdom—*sapientia genita*. To be wise with the wisdom of Christ, we must let Christ be born and live within us in His own way. He does not come to all in the same way, because we all have different functions in His Mystical Body. "There are diversities of graces, but the same Spirit, and there are diversities of ministries but the same Lord: and there are diversities of operations, but the same God Who worketh all in all. And the manifestation of the Spirit is given to every man unto profit." (I Corinthians 12:4-7).

We may apply the last words of this text to our present case. If the Christian poet is truly a Christian poet, if he has a vocation to make known to other men the unsearchable mystery of the love of Christ, then he must do so in the Spirit of Christ. And his "manifestation of the Spirit" not only springs from a kind of contemplative intuition of the mystery of Christ, but is "given to him for his profit" and will therefore deepen and perfect his union with Christ. The Christian poet and artist is one who grows not only by his contemplation but also by his open declaration of the mercy of God. If it is clear that he is called to give this witness to God, then he can say with St. Paul:

"Woe to me if I preach not the Gospel." At the same time, he should always remember that the hidden and more spiritual gifts are infinitely greater than his art, and if he is called upon to make an exclusive choice of one or the other, he must know how to sacrifice his art.

INDEX OF FIRST LINES